Steelers
GLORY

Steelers
GLORY

FOR THE LOVE
OF BRADSHAW,
BIG BEN, AND
THE BUS

ALAN ROSS

CUMBERLAND HOUSE
NASHVILLE, TENNESSEE

STEELERS GLORY
PUBLISHED BY CUMBERLAND HOUSE PUBLISHING, INC.
431 Harding Industrial Drive
Nashville, TN 37211-3160

Cover design: Gore Studio, Inc.
Text design: John Mitchell
Research assistance/data entry: Caroline Ross

Content was compiled from a variety of sources and appears as originally presented; thus, some factual errors and differences in accounts may exist.

Library of Congress Cataloging-in-Publication Data

Ross, Alan.
  Steelers glory : for the love of Bradshaw, Big Ben, and the Bus / Alan Ross.
     p. cm.
  Includes bibliographical references and index.
  ISBN-13: 978-1-58182-538-1 (pbk. : alk. paper)
  ISBN-10: 1-58182-538-2 (pbk. : alk. paper)
  1. Pittsburgh Steelers (Football team)—History. I. Title.

  GV956.P57R66 2006
  796.332'640974886—dc22

                                            2006024572

Printed in the United States of America

1 2 3 4 5 6 7—12 11 10 09 08 07 06

For Jacob, Zach, and Ben Harris,
all born to the great
Black & Gold fraternity

and

for Caroline, their mother,
my constant love

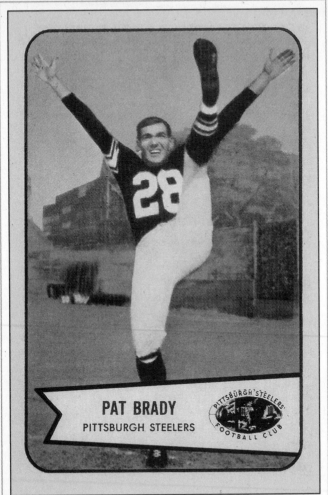

PAT BRADY
PITTSBURGH STEELERS

Pat Brady

CONTENTS

FOREWORD

My introduction to Pittsburgh Steelers football came through no common route. As a kid growing up in southern New England in the early 1950s, Pittsburgh was viewed as a veritable outpost, a western settlement at that.

It was a most exceptional occurrence in the early 1950s to catch a broadcast of a football game, a game of any kind, on TV. One day while flipping through the channels of my folks' almost-brand-new black & white RCA television, my hand froze on the knob as, shocker of shockers, on came a football game, an NFL game as I shortly found out, in which Pittsburgh was playing.

Amazingly, more than fifty years later, my hardening grey matter still retains one particular play from that TV game—a Steelers punt.

A left-footed kicker, wearing one of those goofy, round, cardboard-looking type pieces of head gear, lined up to receive the snap from center. He swung his arms loosely, waiting. The punter palmed the ball high with his left hand, let it drop perfectly flat, then swung through the spheroid with perfect rhythm.

The opposing safetyman positioned deep to receive the kick suddenly turned his back to the oncoming downfield surge in an effort to keep up with the cannonaded punt. It rocketed high over his head and wasn't captured until the beaten returner fell on the ball some twenty-five yards deeper than where he had originally set up.

Pat Brady, that supernova-like left-footer who won two NFL punting titles (1953–54) in three seasons before blowing out an Achilles tendon that prematurely ended a sterling pro career in the Steel City, owns the distinction of being the first Steeler to turn my head.

As I began to assemble *Steelers Glory*, the recollection of that long ago game still brought on a smile. As any football enthusiast of moderate knowledge knows, there have been many more lasting Steelers memories to add to Brady's gargantuan punts of the early- to mid-fifties.

That said, proceed to smear on some black and gold face paint and twirl that Terrible Towel. You're headed for the gritty land of Bullet Bill and Big Ben, The Bomb and The Bus, Whizzer and Wagner, Bam and Ham, Mean Joe and Franco.

Where it's Steelers time all the time.

REMEMBRANCE

The long shadows of a cold mid-December day fell diagonally across the west end zone of old Yankee Stadium. It was still early afternoon, and while much of the stadium's capacity crowd of over 60,000 sat in relative comfort, if northern wintry sunshine can be called comfortable, those of us in the dank bowels of the west end zone grimly steeled ourselves for another three-hour deep freeze.

I was in the first year of my now 44 years-and-counting tenure as a New York Giants season ticket-holder. At that time I was the rarest oddity among the city's boisterous Giants empire: a dedicated non-Giants fan; indeed a fan of all Giants opponents, a fact not lost on my surrounding section mates. As a working college freshman, even I could afford season tickets then, a $75 bargain for 14 games.

That particular afternoon of December 15, 1963, one of the galaxy's all-time rarities awaited the visiting Pittsburgh Steelers should they happen to beat New York: a coveted Eastern Division crown. The flags atop the stadium nearly flapped off their poles from the intermittent wind gusts spasmodically cavorting around the hallowed venue, an ominous portent for Pittsburgh, then looking for its first-ever title of any kind.

These were the waning Giants from their big championship era—the Y.A. Tittle, Del Shofner, Frank Gifford, Sam Huff, Andy Robustelli years that produced six Eastern Division titles and one world championship in eight seasons. Pittsburgh had wondrously slid into the title picture on the basis of a modest 7–3–3 record, the ties mathematically crucial to its prize chance at season's end. But it was to be a tough afternoon.

The Steelers fumbled the first play from scrimmage, the Giants recovered. New York kicked a field goal, Pittsburgh shanked one. With the score still at a manageable 3–0 deficit in the first quarter, I jumped to my feet (yes, the only person standing in the entire section) as the Steelers' Gary Ballman took an Ed Brown pass and churned toward a sure touchdown.

Inexplicably, Ballman dropped the ball near the goal line without a hand being laid on him, as New York defensive back Erich Barnes headed back upfield, a thief with a gift fumble recovery. At the time, a TD would've given Pittsburgh a 7–3 lead. Shortly thereafter, the imperturbable Tittle hit the will o' the wisp Shofner for a long touchdown, and it was quickly 9–0, then 16–0, before Lou Michaels mercifully put three points on the board for Steeltown with seven seconds left in the first half.

The rest of that disappointing day was lost amid a blur of waffling Ed Brown pass attempts, the Pittsburgh QB overmatched not so much by the Giants' defense as by maddening 35-mph wind gusts. Brown's aerials often dove into the hard Bronx dirt five yards short of their intended mark, punctuating another long afternoon of crushed Steelers dreams. In the stands, I nursed what surely had to be a budding case of frostbite and took the traditional verbal abuse from surrounding Giants fans like, well, a young man.

As Pittsburghers were wont to note back then, it had been standard SOS: same old Steelers. Head coach Buddy Parker would later lament that New York's 33–17 victory that day might have had a different outcome had he, Parker, not urged his longtime warrior and master field general Bobby Layne to retire after the previous season.

An interminable decade still separated that frigid afternoon in New York from the glittering dynasty years of the seventies, a passage that ultimately would bring long-awaited jubilation to a long-downtrodden Pittsburgh, releasing it, finally, from the captivity of the previously barren 40 years.

— *A.R.*

1

STEELERS TRADITION

The roads traveled by the Steelers since Art Rooney purchased a National Football League franchise in 1933, is the stuff of incredulity. Can it be that for more than six decades the Steelers, a near-worthless investment that lived to enchant a nation, have been governed by only two men—Art Rooney Sr. and his son Dan? The hurly-burly environment of pro sports has slapped tradition silly, but in Pittsburgh tradition survives.

Myron Cope
longtime Steelers radio broadcaster (1970–2004)

When he started the club during the Depression, in 1933, everybody was on the breadline. He kept the Steelers going. The genius was to keep them in business—not to win or lose, but to stay in business.

> **Art Rooney Jr.**
> *Steelers vice president/director of player personnel (1964–86), on his father's tribulations in the early NFL*

◇ ◇ ◇

He dealt with people like no one I've ever seen. He made you feel as if the most important thing he had to do was to talk to you. He made you feel as if you were a friend. It wasn't planned, and it wasn't calculated.

> **Dan Rooney**
> *Steelers president (1975–2002)/ chairman of the board (2003–), on his father, Art Rooney*

You talk about a true monarch. The thing that is still amazing about that man is that he didn't care if you were Joe Greene or the guy who'd never get in the game, he treated you the same. It was contagious to all of us.

Mel Blount
*cornerback (1970–83),
on The Chief*

To everyone he was simply The Chief, a name cribbed by his twin sons Pat and John from the popular *Superman* television series of the 1950s, leaked to the world, but never used to his face.

Abby Mendelson
*writer/author,
on Art Rooney*

Forty years of losers, and he hated to lose. He was the greatest horseplayer of his time, and he knew how to win. And he was no fool in the business of football. The big thing was to survive. You traded guys to lighten the payroll. He became a master at that.

Art Rooney Jr.
on his father

From day one, my father set the tone on how the Steelers operate. He has always said that what the people think is important, and that we have to think that way. He very much felt that everyone was his equal and that they should be treated that way—players, coaches, girls in the office, everybody. You must treat people with respect.

Dan Rooney

He made time for everybody. He was a folk hero, and he worked at it. And the secret was, he didn't let you know he was working at it.

Art Rooney Jr.
on his dad

◇　◇　◇

My father was a very charitable person. Money meant nothing to him. Values were important.

Dan Rooney

◇　◇　◇

It really made you feel good about how he helped mold and build the NFL. He always had good things to say, encouraging words, and a pat on the back. It was really wonderful, because leadership is everything. You can tell an organization by how the people conduct themselves at the top.

Franco Harris
running back (1972–83),
on Art Rooney

I always looked upon him as a special person. That was the edge we had as a football team. The Cowboys, the Raiders, all of those people were equal to us in terms of talent. The edge that we had was Mr. Rooney. We did it for The Chief.

Joe Greene
defensive tackle (1969–81)

Art Rooney was truly a legend; a larger-than-life figure who was blessed with the common touch. A man called "The Chief" who never once acted the part.

Steve Halvonik
writer

Cigars and stories. That's what I think of when I think of Mr. Rooney. He was always telling stories. And the miracle of it is, he never told the same story twice.

Lynn Swann
wide receiver (1974–82)

Art Rooney is the greatest man who ever walked.

Terry Bradshaw
quarterback (1970–83)

◇   ◇   ◇

The Depression was the time when Pittsburgh began a time-honored, 30-year tradition of blowing the draft. In 1939, the club traded their number-one pick to Chicago. The Steelers got journeyman end Edgar "Eggs" Manske, who played only one season, and the Bears took Sid Luckman and became the Monsters of the Midway.

Abby Mendelson

◇   ◇   ◇

One thing was consistent in Pittsburgh —it was always a good time to rebuild.

Tom Danyluk
writer/Professional Football Researchers Association member, on the 1958–67 decade in Pittsburgh, in which the Steelers, with 70 draft choices in the first seven rounds, only managed to utilize 26 of the selections, frittering away the rest on mostly poor acquisitions

We were always trading away our future and getting players other teams didn't want. That had to stop or we were never going to get better. I don't think we had more than one complete draft between 1958 and 1970.

Art Rooney Jr.

The Depression Steelers were what one former club official called "small potatoes, a hustle." Bought on a day that will live in . . . obscurity, the Depression team was little more than a succession of sandlot teams, cronies, locals, and college boys back before getting on with their life's work. The names are largely forgettable, except for one William Shakespeare, late of Notre Dame, the club's all-time number-one draft choice, who had the good sense not to play.

Abby Mendelson

Although the memorable 1933-edition uniforms had the city seal on them—a shameless tug at civic pride—the players inside were ultimately forgettable; Corwan Artman, Angelo Brovelli, Elmer Schwartz, the names trail off into obscurity. The coach was Forrest "Jap" Douds, and with a 3–6–2 record he lasted but one season.

Abby Mendelson

on Art Rooney's first-year entry into the NFL, the Pittsburgh Pirates

Legend has it that Margaret Carr, wife of ticketmeister and longtime Rooney aide-de-camp Joe Carr, proposed the new name in the spring of 1941.

Abby Mendelson

on the name change of the Pittsburgh Pirates to the Pittsburgh Steelers

> **FAST FACT:** Some pro football reference sources cite 1940 as the year the name change occurred.

Only a world war ever produced a football team as odd as the Phil-Pitt Steagles.

Tom Infield

writer, Philadelphia Inquirer, *on the wartime hookup of the Eagles and Steelers to cut operating costs. The mixed conglomerate went a surprising 5–4–1*

◇ ◇ ◇

Greasy Neale and Walt Kiesling were able to meld the Steagles into an effective team. Going into their final game, which they lost to the Green Bay Packers, they had a chance to tie for the Eastern Division title.

Tom Infield

◇ ◇ ◇

In 1944, the last full year of war, the Steelers merged with the Chicago Cardinals. That team was so bad, 0–10, that writers called it the Car-Pitts—the carpets— because everybody walked all over them.

Tom Infield

Merging made us twice as bad as we had been by ourselves.

> **Art Rooney**
> *Steelers founding owner and president (1933–74)/chairman of the board (1933–88), on the wartime collaborations of the 1943 Philadelphia Eagles-Pittsburgh Steelers—the Steagles —and the 1944 pairing of the Chicago Cardinals and Pittsburgh that became Card-Pitt. Though the '43 Steagles managed a winning mark of 5–4–1, the ignominious Card-Pitt team went 0–10*

Rooney and Cardinals owner Charlie Bidwill had a collection of eight medically discharged veterans, a number of 4Fs, and several high schoolers.

> **Andrew O'Toole**
> *author, on the makeup of Card-Pitt in 1944*

In [the early 1950s] you played 20 football games, but eight were exhibition games, which you got nothing for. In fact, if you were away to play a Saturday night ball game, and you were going to stay the night, they would give you $5 for dinner and breakfast. $5 for both!

George Hughes

two-time Pro Bowl guard/tackle (1950–54)

◇ ◇ ◇

The Pittsburgh Steelers were the last NFL team to convert from the single wing to the T, in 1952.

Jim Campbell

writer/Professional Football Researchers Association member

◇ ◇ ◇

During my time there the team was a six-month-a-year operation.

Jim Finks

quarterback-defensive back (1949–55)/administrator/ Pro Football Hall of Famer

Hi diddle diddle, Rogel up the middle.

Crowd chant

*mocking head coach Walt Kiesling's
unimaginative play-calling in 1956,
which usually centered around
fullback Fran Rogel (1950–57) on
basic straight-ahead handoffs*

◇   ◇   ◇

Buddy Parker once said that one of these
days the Steelers will get lucky, and when
they do, it'll last for ten years.

Art Rooney

FAST FACT: The clairvoyant Parker, Pittsburgh's head
coach from 1957 through '64, was some soothsayer, for
the decade of the 1970s belonged to the Steelers.

I think it was a combination of things, people, and timing. It was Chuck Noll coming at
the right time, Artie's (Art Rooney, Jr.) work
with personnel, the new stadium. It might
have happened with any one of them—but
it did happen with that combination.

Dan Rooney

*on the phenomenal Steelers
turnaround in the early seventies*

The Steelers' defense of Joe Greene, Jack Lambert, Jack Ham, and Mel Blount was noteworthy in that the secondary hit with the same zeal, power, and aggressiveness that the line and linebackers did.

Jim Campbell

◇ ◇ ◇

You can lose with good football players, but you can never, ever win without them.

Art Rooney Jr.

◇ ◇ ◇

I learned more about this business from coaches than I did from anyone else.

Dan Rooney

◇ ◇ ◇

He's a leader who doesn't want to be a leader. He never promotes himself, and would rather not be in the forefront.

Tunch Ilkin

tackle (1980–92)/Steelers broadcast analyst (1998–), on Dan Rooney

Dan Rooney's never received the credit for what's happened here. Not only has he lived in the shadow of his father, but he's lived in the shadow of Coach Noll. It's a team effort. If you don't have a good solid owner, a guy who has a vision and direction, it doesn't make any difference what else you have. If you don't have a solid person at the top of the organization, you're never going to be successful.

Tom Donahoe
former Steelers director of football operations

When you come to play the Pittsburgh Steelers, you're going to remember it.

Rod Woodson
cornerback/safety/kick returner (1987–96)

We were tough people—and we took great pride in being tough people. I took great pride from being from a smokey, dirty city. That was part of our personality. We're going to smoke your butt and dirty you up.

Dwight White
defensive end (1971–80)

◇ ◇ ◇

I always thought that football in that town reflected life in that town, and that tradition has carried on. Pittsburgh has always repre-sented a team that is proud of its hard-nosed past.

Ray Mansfield
center (1964–76)

◇ ◇ ◇

Mark Malone was no Terry Bradshaw, and neither was Bubby Brister; Weegie Thomp-son was no Lynn Swann; Frankie Pollard was no Franco Harris. And no man of woman born was Joe Greene.

Abby Mendelson
as the Steelers moved into the 1980s

We continually try to get the right kind of people that fit together. This is such a group effort that I don't think any one individual should be accountable for the large degree of success or failure. It's an organizational attempt to win a championship. We're all in this thing together. That's the bottom line. We win as one, and we lose as one.

Bill Cowher
head coach (1992–)

◇　◇　◇

A Steelers opponent once said, "They start trapping you when you get off the team bus." This is a reference to the kind of line blocking that sprung Pittsburgh runners loose—from the Chuck Noll era (Franco Harris) through the Bill Cowher era (Barry Foster, Bam Morris, and Jerome Bettis).

Jim Campbell

I knew we'd win if I lived long enough. I did get kind of worried as it got later in my life.

Art Rooney

then 71, after his Steelers beat San Diego, 24–2, to win their first-ever crown of any kind, ending 40 frustrating years, with the 1972 AFC Central Division title

Some franchises don't have the same owner for seven months. The Rooneys have led the Steelers for over seventy years with no intention of relinquishing the reins. They neither boast nor berate; like our mountains and rivers, they simply are, and are so good at what they do, we tend to take them for granted. We shouldn't.

Abby Mendelson

My dad loved that football team.

Art Rooney Jr.

on "The Chief"

THE BLACK & GOLD

*F*ourteen players who wore the Black & Gold, one legendary coach who orchestrated them, and two Rooneys—the founding Arthur and his top executive son, Dan—have been enshrined in the Pro Football Hall of Fame. And while the immortal Steelers—Bradshaw, Harris, Stautner, Greene, Lambert, Ham, and the rest—produced countless great moments, the toiling of the merely mortal day-to-day players who generated far less press dot the historic landscape of Pittsburgh Steelers football. A few may still gain a Hall of Fame nod one day, but like the blue-collar pride that permeates the Steel City at the confluence of the three rivers, these players took on their tasks in true blue-collar fashion, integral cogs all.

Army great Doc Blanchard was the Steelers' first-round draft pick in 1946, but the 1945 Heisman Trophy winner never played a down of pro football.

Ed Bouchette
longtime Steelers
beat writer/author

◇ ◇ ◇

With a good team, he would have been as good as anybody—Otto Graham or any of them.

Fran Fogarty
former Steelers
business manager,
on 1950s quarterback Jim Finks

◇ ◇ ◇

Lynn Chandnois made his debut in 1950, then provided the Steelers their best all-around offensive threat for seven seasons. He was a running back, receiver, kick returner, punt returner, and occasional passer.

Abby Mendelson
on the Steelers' two-time
Pro Bowl halfback

If my horses could go that fast I'd be a wealthy man!

Art Rooney
*on early 1950s halfback/
kick returner Lynn Chandnois*

I cut Chandnois, because Walt Kiesling (preceding Steelers head coach) suggested I do something drastic to recover the team. It had gotten away from Kiesling. How I regretted that decision. As I went over the game films, it came to me what a great runner Lynn Chandnois was. If I had known that, I never would have let him go.

Buddy Parker
*head coach (1957–64),
after inexplicably cutting the
Steelers' fine halfback before
Parker's first season as head
coach, in 1957*

During George Hughes's five years, the Steelers had nobody better at offensive guard or tackle. Only one Steeler made the Pro Bowl more than twice: linebacker Jerry Shipkey (1951, 1952, 1953).

Jim Sargent

writer/Professional Football Researchers Association member, on the Steelers' two-time Pro Bowl guard/tackle from 1950 through '54

George Hughes was a great player. He had the quickness, the speed, and the strength to hit hard and do a terrific job of blocking. But he never really got the recognition he deserved, which certainly was not helped by playing for Pittsburgh.

Lou Creekmur

Detroit Lions Hall of Fame tackle (1950–59)

George Hughes's career represents the best of the NFL's unsung heroes from the pre–1960 era: the rugged linemen who fought weekly battles on the violent fronts of pro football.

Jim Sargent

When I came in 1955, Pittsburgh had Fran Rogel at fullback. Lynn Chandnois was their most effective halfback. He was smooth, and he had great athletic ability. Jimmy Finks was the quarterback, and Ted Marchibroda was the backup.

Frank Varrichione
offensive tackle (1955–60)

Frank Varrichione was every bit as good an offensive tackle as any in the league.

Lynn Chandnois
halfback (1950–56)

I respected Frank's leadership and his courage on the field, and also his knowledge of how to hold without getting caught. Frank had "the best hands in the business."

Merlin Olsen
*Los Angeles Rams Hall of Fame
defensive tackle,
on Varrichione*

There may have been an even better punter than the Cleveland Browns' Horace Gillom in the early- to mid-'50s, though you won't find his name among the league's official all-time top 10 punters list. His name was Pat Brady, a left-footed kicker for the Pittsburgh Steelers who first showed his skills in front of Art Rooney and the Steelers at their 1952 summer camp with an end zone-to-end zone jaw dropper.

NFL Insider

FAST FACT: Brady would lead the NFL in punting two of his three years in the league, before suffering a career-ending torn Achilles tendon in his kicking leg during the 1955 preseason, denying the Steelers and kicking fans everywhere further appreciation of his prodigious talent.

Contrary to what some writers state, Big Daddy Lipscomb did not invent "pursuit." He was just good at it at a time when too few players bothered to play sideline-to-sideline.

Jim Campbell

on the Steelers' behemoth defensive tackle (1961–62)

Big Daddy did three things: he drank, he screwed, and he dominated football games.

Brady Keys

defensive back (1961–67), on teammate and 300-pound defensive tackle Eugene "Big Daddy" Lipscomb, who died of acute heroin poisoning in 1963

I was the last of a dying breed, a slow white running back. I didn't have all the talent in the world, so I had to get every edge that I could. I had to study the game. I had to know what everyone else was doing on the field.

Dick Hoak
halfback (1961–70)/assistant coach (1972–)

FAST FACT: Hoak is the longest tenured coach in NFL history, entering his 35th season on the Steelers sidelines in 2006.

◇   ◇   ◇

He was the most perfect player in my time.

Bobby Layne
*quarterback (1958–62),
on halfback Dick Hoak*

With the recognition of Mike Webster (9) and more recently Dermontti Dawson (7), the Steelers' centers have been well-treated by the Pro Bowl. But Webster's predecessor, Ray Mansfield, played for some very poor Pittsburgh teams and so was overlooked at Pro Bowl time. His most notable achievement was his streak of 196 consecutive games played, but his steadiness never translated into post-season honors.

Mike Sparrow
writer/Professional Football Researchers Association member, on one of his "All-Time Non Pro Bowl Team" selections

I prided myself in being able to know the opponents. I knew what they were going to do before they did.

Andy Russell
linebacker (1963, 1966–76)

Andy Russell? The ultimate intellectual.

Dan Rooney

If one area of the great Steelers teams was overlooked when it came to Pro Bowl honors, it was their offensive line. Until the emergence of Mike Webster in the late seventies, only one offensive lineman (guard Bruce Van Dyke, in 1974) was chosen for the Pro Bowl.

Mike Sparrow

on his "All-Time Non Pro Bowl Team"

FAST FACT: While Van Dyke was the only offensive lineman preceding Webster in the 1970s as a Pro Bowler, seven different Steeler OLs were selected in the 1950s and '60s.

When he got back, he looked like something that had come out of a concentration camp. But the kid wanted to play.

Ralph Berlin

former Steelers trainer,
on Rocky Bleier, impaired by
several war injuries, returning for
his first Steelers training camp
following service in Vietnam

Rocky Bleier began his career with Pittsburgh in 1968 but it was interrupted by service in Vietnam. A severe foot injury there sidetracked his career, but he persevered and rejoined a much better Steelers team in 1971. Though he gained 1,036 yards in 1976, Bleier never had the rushing numbers of Franco Harris. But he was a much better blocking back and was strong in the clutch, as proven by his six postseason touchdowns.

Mike Sparrow

on another one of his "All-Time Non Pro Bowl Team" selections

Rocky Bleier began as a "third guard" (a reference to his superb blocking) before given an opportunity to carry the ball significantly.

Jim Campbell

He broke all the rules. He shouldn't have been playing. He shouldn't have been on the team. What can you say? You can't measure the heart or the head.

Jack Butler
*defensive back (1951–59),
on Rocky Bleier*

◇　◇　◇

Ernie Holmes—his motive was to hurt somebody.

J. T. Thomas
*defensive back (1973–77,
1979–81)*

◇　◇　◇

Ernie Holmes was great against the run.

John Hannah
*New England Patriots
Hall of Fame guard,
on DLs that gave him the most
trouble*

You had the smart guys back there in that secondary—Mike Wagner, who was probably the most unsung hero of our football team. . . . To this day, Roger Staubach still complains that Wagner guessed on the play for an interception in the Super Bowl X. I always tell Roger, "You know, you gotta let it go. It's over." You need smart guys back there.

Jack Ham
linebacker (1971–82)

The Steelers got a lot of unshakable cool from a kid quarterback with the poise of a flim-flam man.

Phil Musick
writer,
on rookie quarterback "Jefferson Street Joe" Gilliam, 1972

Jefferson Street Joe Gilliam was talented and tragic. He wasn't a dumbbell at all but he had little common sense. We had one of the all-time great defenses and a Hall of Fame runner in Franco Harris, but all Joe wanted to do was toss the ball. He got the defense in trouble a lot. Bradshaw worked his way back into the starting lineup by listening to Chuck Noll. Terry played the team's strengths. Joey was too impatient to do that. He was all downfield, a mad bomber.

Art Rooney Jr.

*on the Steelers' quarterback
of the early to mid-seventies,
who eventually lost his place
in the league, and later his life,
from repeated misuse of drugs*

When I think about things that happened on the football field, my body starts aching. I can feel that pain. One thing I always wanted: to be able to play one game when I wasn't hurt. But it didn't happen. I never played a game that my ankle or my shoulder or my knee or my back or my hand wasn't hurt.

L. C. Greenwood
defensive end (1969–81)

We'd line up and say, "Meet you at the quarterback."

L. C. Greenwood
*the Steelers' all-time leader
in sacks, with 73.5,
on his front-four linemates
Ernie Holmes, Joe Greene, and
Dwight White*

The only thing I know about offense is "Full right, 19 straight."

Jon Kolb

*offensive tackle (1969–81),
on one of the Steelers' bread-and-butter running plays for Franco Harris in the 1970s*

◇　◇　◇

Pound for pound the toughest player for us was Glen Edwards, the free safety. I remember he hit the Vikings' John Gilliam on a crossing route down by the goal line in Super Bowl IX—just drilled him on the chin. Today, he'd have been fined $25,000 for that hit.

Jack Ham

◇　◇　◇

Merril Hoge breaks more tackles than Manuel Noriega breaks laws.

Steve Hubbard

writer

I've seen guys run for a lot more yards, but I've never seen anybody run for yards that tough. As much yardage as he got, it was all hard yards. Even when there were people in the holes, he was running over them. Breaking tackle after tackle.

Dick Hoak

on running back Merril Hoge, who bulldozed for 120 yards on 16 carries and corralled eight passes for another 60 yards in an AFC divisional playoff loss to Denver, January 7, 1990

At six-foot-five and 275 pounds, he was simply a huge target that was too good to be true—and too big to miss.

Abby Mendelson

on tight end Eric Green (1990–94)

It makes me proud to be compared with the best receivers Pittsburgh's ever had. But I can't agree that we're the best ever. Maybe the best season for a group of wide receivers. But until we go out and do it year after year, consecutively, we can't be compared to those guys.

Yancy Thigpen
*wide receiver (1992–97),
on the Steelers' 1995 receiver
corps, which included Ernie
Mills, Andre Hastings, Charles
Johnson, and occasionally
quarterback Kordell Stewart,
in comparison to the dynasty
tandem of Swann-Stallworth*

Greg Lloyd alone is a one-man wrecking crew—Pro Bowl outside linebacker, devastating belter, and blitzer par excellence. At college, he majored in intensity, velocity, and unapologetic violence.

Abby Mendelson
*on the Steelers linebacker from
1988 through 1997*

He's very strong and quick, a physical player who doesn't fear anything. He throws his body around like he's not worried about any injury or any consequence. Two linemen come at him, he doesn't think twice about blowing through them for the ball carrier. It's almost as if Greg has turned off the switch and is running on pure emotion. We feed off Greg Lloyd.

Carnell Lake
strong safety (1989–98)

We didn't care what the offense did. We were hoping the offense would go out there and throw an interception or fumble the ball so we could get back on the field. But, you've got to have a good defense to have that kind of confidence.

Greg Lloyd
linebacker (1988–97)

He's just ruthless—and about as tough as they come.

Barry Foster
running back (1990–94),
on Greg Lloyd

◇　◇　◇

He's the ultimate warrior. He's big, strong, and fast. He's the best strong safety in the game.

Ernie Mills
on four-time Pro Bowl strong
safety Carnell Lake

◇　◇　◇

Bright guy, hard hitter, Carnell will just tag you.

Tunch Ilkin

◇　◇　◇

I'm capable of doing a lot of things, but I'm a quarterback. I've said that, and I always will say that. That Slash thing, that's fine and dandy. But I'm Kordell Stewart, and I'm a quarterback.

Kordell Stewart
quarterback/wide receiver/
running back/punter (1995–2002)

Everyone talks about Elway and Marino, Elway and Marino. Tonight you saw another great—Neil O'Donnell.

Ron Erhardt

*Steelers offensive coordinator (1992–95),
on O'Donnell's 341-yard, two-touchdown passing effort in a come-from-behind overtime win over the Chicago Bears, November 5, 1995, at Soldier Field*

◇ ◇ ◇

I had to prove myself as a blocker or else I wasn't going to catch anything.

Heath Miller

*tight end (2005–),
on his job description as a first-year Steeler. Miller caught just two passes his first month with Pittsburgh, as he learned blocking assignments and refined his technique. By season's end, he wound up with 39 receptions and six touchdowns*

He is the best quarterback prospect I have seen in 10 or 15 years. I have not seen anybody come into the league like that. The only guy that I can say came in, and the first year started playing like he is playing, is Dan Marino.

Bill Parcells
*Dallas Cowboys head coach,
on Ben Roethlisberger*

◇　◇　◇

The kid is riding an all-time high.

Hines Ward
*wide receiver (1998–)/
Super Bowl XL MVP/Steelers
all-time receptions leader,
on Roethlisberger*

◇　◇　◇

You can't describe his effort, and he's earning a lot of respect on this team. The guys on this team are fighting hard for him.

Hines Ward
on Ben Roethlisberger

AP / WIDE WORLD PHOTO

Ben Roethlisberger

Big Ben, he's growing up real fast. The clock has struck all the right numbers for him, man.

Cedrick Wilson
wide receiver (2005–)

◇ ◇ ◇

The thing that's impressive about Ben is his awareness in the pocket, his pocket presence and his ability to move and still make throws downfield. You can't teach those kind of instincts. That's something he has going for him that a lot of the guys in the league don't have.

Dan Marino
Miami Dolphins Hall of Fame quarterback, on Ben Roethlisberger

◇ ◇ ◇

I want the ball in my hands. I want to have control of the outcome of the game.

Ben Roethlisberger
quarterback (2004–)

It's scary to think how much better he might get.

Hines Ward
on Big Ben

◇ ◇ ◇

The way he throws on the run, being able to stop and sling it 40–50 yards, that's just natural ability.

Jeff Hartings
center (2001–),
on Roethlisberger

◇ ◇ ◇

His two-year QB rating of 98.3 is the best to open a career since some guy named Marino. Plus, Big Ben has won 88 percent of his starts, and his Steelers won the Super Bowl. Oh yeah, he's done all this while learning that less (just 22 passes per game) is more.

Elena Bergeron
ESPN The Magazine,
on Ben Roethlisberger

The thing I like about him, he has a good perspective on things. He doesn't get caught up in it, maybe because of where he has come from. I can't say enough about Tommy. He epitomizes what this team is all about.

Bill Cowher
on quarterback Tommy Maddox

FAST FACT: After apparently failing in the NFL after being the No. 1 pick of the Denver Broncos in 1992, the man selected to eventually replace John Elway journeyed on to five other NFL teams, played in the Arena Football League, the defunct XFL, and was even out of the game entirely for three years. Signed by the Steelers as a backup for the 2001 season, Maddox replaced an ineffective Kordell Stewart in early 2002 and wound up earning the NFL Comeback Player of the Year award. The following season, he was frighteningly paralyzed from a hit during a game with the Tennessee Titans, temporarily losing all feeling in his legs. Three weeks later, he was back starting at QB again for Pittsburgh.

You have to work for everything, then enjoy the ride; enjoy life.

Tommy Maddox
quarterback (2001–)

Troy Polamalu is the best big-game defensive player in football. If his diving pick of Peyton Manning hadn't been over-turned, it would have gone down as the greatest interception in Steelers history.

Peter King
Sports Illustrated,
on the strong safety's theft during the Steelers' 2005 AFC divisional playoff win over Indianapolis that was ruled an incomplete pass. The NFL later acknowledged the referee had erred on the call

◇ ◇ ◇

He's sideline to sideline. He plays with one of the highest motors I've ever seen.

Mike Shanahan
*Denver Broncos head coach,
on Troy Polamalu*

◇ ◇ ◇

I feel I should never be blocked. That's just the mentality I have.

Casey Hampton
nose tackle (2001–)

They don't call him "Fast Willie" for nothing. Willie Parker gained that nickname as a rookie and lived up to it by blazing his name into the Super Bowl record book.

Chuck Johnson

USA TODAY,
on Parker's third quarter 75-yard scoring dash that gave Pittsburgh the deciding touchdown in its 21–10 victory over Seattle in Super Bowl XL. Parker's run broke Marcus Allen's previous record for the longest touchdown run in Super Bowl history by a yard

◇ ◇ ◇

He is a force in our locker room. He's somebody that we turn to.

Kimo von Oelhoffen

defensive end (2000–05), on outside linebacker Joey Porter

3

STEELERS
CHARACTER

When Columbus got on that boat, a lot of people told him, "Don't get on it; the world is flat." He just kept going. He found land. I told our team: "There's a lot of people who tell you that you can't do it. That doesn't mean you don't go try." History is not going to determine our fate. Our effort today made history.

Bill Cowher

after the Steelers' "One for the Thumb" victory in Super Bowl XL

There's just no feeling like collectively doing something to be the best, and sharing that feeling with others.

"Iron Mike" Webster
center (1974–88)

Bobby Layne had football character. He was never late for practice. He was always there early and stayed late, and some guys followed his lead. After the season was over, I sat down and added up all his extra practice time. I couldn't believe it! Layne had practiced an entire month longer than the rest of the team. Now that's football character.

Art Rooney Jr.
on the legendary Hall of Fame quarterback who guided the Steelers from 1958 through '62

I don't care if they only throw one pass to me the whole game. I'll make sure that I catch that one.

Lynn Swann

◇ ◇ ◇

Treat everybody the way you'd like to be treated. Give them the benefit of the doubt. But never let anyone mistake kindness for weakness.

Art Rooney

◇ ◇ ◇

He's the voice of the man in the street.

Cardinal John L. Wright
on Art Rooney

◇ ◇ ◇

There aren't too many football owners who would have sat still for some of the things I've said about the Steelers. When they're good, I enjoy it. But when they stink, I say it. They never tried to censor or put a muzzle on me.

Myron Cope

They gave me that extra shot. That was the character of the men. Here was a kid, former altar boy, Notre Dame halfback, called into service, got wounded, and came back. All heart, with not a whole lot of talent. They gave me a second—and third—chance. That's the way of the Rooneys—that's the way Art was, and that's the way Dan is.

Rocky Bleier
running back (1968, 1970–80)

Talk about tough. You'd beat on Jim Finks all day, but he wouldn't back off. I loved him for that.

Frank "Bucko" Kilroy
*Philadelphia Eagles three-time
Pro Bowl tackle,
on Pittsburgh's 5–10, 175-pound
QB of the early- to mid–1950s,
a future Hall of Famer*

God takes care of fools and babies, and I wasn't a baby. I had a lot of pride and made a big contribution that year (1974). The bottom line—it was too big a game to miss.

Dwight White

who, suffering from pleurisy that had turned into pneumonia, left a hospital bed to suit up for Super Bowl IX. White stunned Steelers coaches with a dynamic performance, going the distance at defensive end in the 16–6 victory over Minnesota. Mission accomplished, White reportedly returned to the hospital after the game

◇　◇　◇

He played like a guy going into a burning house after his family.

George Perles

defensive line coach (1972–81), on convalescing Dwight "Mad Dog" White's courageous performance in Super Bowl IX

My attitude was always, "Never say die, never be defeated. Go down fighting on the beach."

Ray Mansfield

◇ ◇ ◇

You come to Pittsburgh, don't even try it. You're going to lose the game, and we're going to dominate it. It was almost arrogance, but Dizzy Dean said, "It ain't braggin' if you can do it." And we did it.

Dwight White

◇ ◇ ◇

Never carry on like a big shot.

Art Rooney

◇ ◇ ◇

You get nothing out of life unless you get it with the help of other people. How unique it is to go through this experience together, with all these people who were put together. It's amazing. I'm very proud.

Terry Bradshaw

You do what you have to do.

Rocky Bleier

◇ ◇ ◇

Losing is a greater learning experience than winning. You have to be able to handle success, but you have to be able to overcome failure. It's not a sin to fail.

Chuck Noll

head coach (1969–91)

◇ ◇ ◇

It's not a sin to get knocked down, but it is a sin to stay down.

Mike Webster

◇ ◇ ◇

If you don't force yourself too much, or put too much pressure on yourself, if you let things flow, it gets to be fun.

Carnell Lake

◇ ◇ ◇

They can't beat us. And we ain't gonna beat ourselves. That's the name of the game.

Greg Lloyd

If you don't have a love for the game, and you don't appreciate the game, and you don't take the game seriously enough, it's not going to happen. No matter what you do.

Rod Woodson

I'm a gunslinger, not a mailman.

Terry Bradshaw
to teammate Tunch Ilkin, who thought the Steelers' plan was to run rather than pass during their 34–7 division-crown-winning effort over the New York Jets, December 10, 1983—Bradshaw's final game. With shredded ligaments in the elbow of his throwing arm, Bradshaw still managed to throw two TD passes in his Pittsburgh swan song

A great player can physically make a great play against you, and you can chalk it up to that guy having great physical talent. But a mental error, where your mistake costs the game or a touchdown, makes you think, "Did I prepare well enough? How come I made that error?" You feel like you've let your teammates down.

Jack Ham

That we could knock 'em out, lay 'em out with one blow; that we were intimidating physically, some may say that we were. But I think our real character and the fingerprint we left on the game was that we were persistently on top of our game.

Joe Greene

The thing I pride myself on is that I've been able to come back. It's a great feeling to face adversity, overcome it, and rise to the top.

Terry Bradshaw
who twice lost his starting job, once in the 1974 preseason and once during the regular season following a loss to Cincinnati

You only find out what someone is all about when the game is in their hands. Let him (the quarterback) make the crucial call. Especially with the money they pay these men. . . . You tell me they can't learn these plays and learn these defenses and what works against them? All they have to do is study and prepare and understand it.

Terry Bradshaw
on calling plays from the sideline

Everyone expected us to lose the first game. Everyone expected us to lose the second game. Everyone expected us to lose this game. We had each other's backs the whole way. Sometimes that's all you want is each other.

Ben Roethlisberger

on the Steelers' eye-popping 3–0 playoff victory trail in 2005 at Cincinnati, Indianapolis, and Denver that led to Super Bowl XL. The road-warrior trifecta enabled Pittsburgh to become the first team to beat the No. 1-, 2-, and 3-seeded teams in consecutive weeks to reach a Super Bowl

I don't sugarcoat anything. If you don't say how you feel, you're never going to tell the truth. And the truth might not be what everybody wants to hear.

Joey Porter

outside linebacker (1999–)

No one knows another man's pain.

Joe Greene

4

STEELERS HUMOR

I always get kidded mercilessly about my 93-yard fumble recovery against Baltimore in the 1975 playoffs, where I set the NFL record for the most-elapsed time in a single play. I picked the ball up and the field tilted; I was running uphill. Ray Mansfield said NBC cut to a commercial and came back in time to see me run into the end zone.

Andy Russell

How you doin', Mike? How's everything going? That's a good Irish name, Michael.

Art Rooney

to 1980s three-time Pro Bowl linebacker Mike Merriweather, an African American

We laughed when Jack Lambert suggested they put skirts on quarterbacks.

Jack Clary

author

Well now, he's not a member of Mensa; let's not get carried away.

Jack Ham

on the "smart" play of Steel Curtain safety Mike Wagner

On the eve of his final game in 1962, Bobby Layne nodded off at the wheel of his car and collided with what he later described as a "parked, swerving streetcar." Though bloodied in the crash, he played the entire game the next day.

Austin Murphy
writer

The Steelers were going back to the Super Bowl for the first time since the 1979 season, and that could mean only three things: Grown men wearing hard hats with beer cans on top. Women knitting black-and-gold sweaters. Polka music with Steeler lyrics.

Gerry Dulac
Pittsburgh Post-Gazette,
on the euphoria surrounding Pittsburgh's appearance in Super Bowl XXX

I just wrap my arms around the whole backfield and peel 'em one by one until I get to the ball carrier. Him I keep.

Eugene "Big Daddy" Lipscomb
defensive tackle (1961–62)

◇　◇　◇

Jack Ham is to the art of linebacking what Hugh Hefner is to girlie magazines.

Phil Musick

◇　◇　◇

I may be dumb, but I'm not stupid.

Terry Bradshaw

◇　◇　◇

Martini for martini, this may be the toughest man ever to play in the NFL. His face, emerging directly from his shoulders without the benefit of a neck, is about as pretty as an auto accident.

Myron Cope
on legendary Steelers defensive tackle Ernie Stautner

I don't want to waste any extra effort. . . . You don't get extra points for length. I've got a few different clubs in my bag. But the bag doesn't have the Tiger Woods 5-iron anymore.

Gary Anderson
kicker (1982–94)

◇ ◇ ◇

Worst beard? Ben Roethlisberger. Why? Just look at it. Does it look good to you? It's awful. Great guy, bad beard.

Chris Hoke
nose tackle (2001–)

If I had done that, I'd look like Gandolf from *Lord of the Rings*.

> **Brett Keisel**
>
> *defensive end/special teams*
> *(2002, 2004–),*
> *asked on Media Day during*
> *Super Bowl XL week if he'd been*
> *growing his beard all season*
> *long in 2005*

A Supreme Court Justice once played in the Steelers backfield. So did a lot of guys whose cases would come before him.

> **Jim Murray**
>
> *legendary sports journalist for*
> *the* Los Angeles Times,
> *on Byron "Whizzer" White*

A writer once asked tackle Bob Gaona (1953–56) why he and teammate Frank Varrichione wore hearing aids in their helmets. "The hearing aids not only permit us to hear the signals more clearly," Gaona replied, "but give a clearer meaning to Chaucer and the sonnets of Shelley when we discuss those subjects in the huddle."

Ray Didinger

author/writer/NFL Films senior producer

That's like putting whitewalls on a dump truck.

Chuck Noll

*to defensive back/special teams player Ray Oldham,
immersed in his pregame ritual
of wrapping white tape around
his football shoes, spats-style*

I think an XL shirt might be a little too small for Jerome, but Super Bowl Forty is a good size for him.

Ben Roethlisberger
on Jerome Bettis

◇　◇　◇

I'm not allowed to comment on lousy referees.

Jim Finks
asked after a loss what he thought of the officiating

◇　◇　◇

I'm so hungry I could eat the south end of a northbound skunk.

Craig Hanneman
defensive end (1972–73)

5

STEELERS LEGENDS

For a while in 1938, The Chief must've thought he had something. To complement the quick and crazy Johnny Blood, he bought one of America's greatest gridiron stars—Byron "Whizzer" White. An All-American out of Colorado, White had accepted a Rhodes Scholarship to study at Oxford. But before taking the boat, he squeezed in one season for the Steelers—for the unheard-of price of $15,000. Although the team went 2–9, White did his job. His 567 yards led the team—and the league.

Abby Mendelson

Johnny Blood (McNally) was the most consistently prolific receiver in the game until the immortal Don Hutson came along and created the mold for the modern-day wide receiver. Blood accomplished all he did as a receiver while playing as a full-time running back and playing defense.

Jim Campbell

I have been exhibited like a freak since I signed with the Pirates. Not that I'm complaining—if I paid a player $15,000, I would exploit him, too. It's tough to play your best game when you feel that nothing short of a 50-yard run or a 75-yard pass will satisfy the customers.

Byron "Whizzer" White
*halfback (1938),
on the future United States
Supreme Court Justice's one
season (1938) with the Pirates*

AP / WIDE WORLD PHOTO

Whizzer White

No player ever was as good as my publicity made me out to be. Well, maybe Dutch Clark. But I'm no Dutch Clark.

Byron "Whizzer" White

crediting the Detroit Lions'
Hall of Fame tailback of the 1930s

Tackler after tackler either missed or bounced off as the great Coloradan made his final gesture at the game which has given him $15,000 for a season of play before he goes to England on a Rhodes scholarship.

Associated Press

December 1938,
referring to Byron "Whizzer"
White's 42-yard run in the closing
seconds of his final game as a
Pittsburgh Pirate, a 13–7 loss to
the Rams in New Orleans. With
the run, White locked up the NFL
rushing title with 567 yards

Whizzer White couldn't carry this boy's shoes. Bill Dudley was the finest back we had in our first ten years in the league.

Art Rooney

◇　◇　◇

He was Mr. Versatility, amassing 8,157 yard in rushing, receptions, and kick returns, scoring 484 points and intercepting 23 passes. He kicked field goals and extra points, punted, and threw passes, too.

Michael Richman

writer/Professional Football Researchers Association member, on the career stats of "Bullet Bill" Dudley, one of only three players in NFL history to record a statistical "triple crown" (Sammy Baugh, Steve Van Buren the others). In 1946, Dudley led the NFL in rushing (604 yards), interceptions (10), and punt returns (27 returns for 385 yards). He later played for Detroit (1947–49) and Washington (1950–51, 1953)

I loved the game of football. I didn't even think about being good, bad, or indifferent. I never concerned myself with whether I was the leading ground gainer or pass interception leader, or anything else. I just played to try to win a ball game.

"Bullet Bill" Dudley
halfback (1942, 1945–46)

> *FAST FACT:* Dudley missed two and a half seasons in his prime (1943 through midseason 1945) due to military service. He was voted league MVP in 1946, his third and final season with the Steelers.

He couldn't do anything with finesse. He was just one of those guys that really got it done.

Dan Rooney
on "Bullet Bill" Dudley, the 5–10, 176-pound running back described by the Pro Football Hall of Fame as "small and slow with an unorthodox running style"

He did everything wrong. He couldn't throw. He was not fast. He was not big. He couldn't kick. But he led the league in ground gained—and in interceptions [in 1946]. He was one of those players—Bill Dudley was intelligent and explosive. He was a winner.

Dan Rooney

on the Hall of Fame Steelers halfback

Walt Kiesling was a tremendous competitor. He loved the game. When Bobby Layne joined the Steelers, he asked Kies how long he had played pro ball. "Until they wouldn't let me suit up anymore," Kiesling replied. And he meant it.

Ray Didinger

Kies was the physical duplicate of Babe Ruth. He was big like Ruth and a left-hander, too. Like Ruth, he played his best when he had some belly on him.

Johnny "Blood" McNally
halfback (1934, 1937–39)/
head coach (1937–39),
on the Steelers' Hall of Fame
guard of 1937–38 and onetime
assistant and head coach

Ernie was one of the NFL's first impact players along the defensive line. He was probably the most well-known player on the team throughout much of his career and one of the greatest players to ever wear a Steelers uniform.

Dan Rooney
on nine-time Pro Bowler and
Hall of Famer Stautner

AP / WIDE WORLD PHOTO

Ernie Stautner

He lifted play to a different level. When they couldn't win anything, he gave you 155 percent.

Myron Cope

on immortal 1950s defensive tackle Ernie Stautner

◇   ◇   ◇

You've got to be a man who wants to hurt somebody. You know where I'm going for? The quarterback's face. It hurts in the face. I want him to know I'm coming the next time. I want him to be scared.

Ernie Stautner

defensive tackle (1950–63)

◇   ◇   ◇

Steelers coaches always said Jack Butler could have been an all-pro receiver but was too valuable to move from defense. He intercepted 52 passes in a 1951–59 career, with four Pro Bowls.

Bob Carroll

historian/author/publisher

Jack Butler was one guy who could have played with the teams of the '70s. He was fast, smart, and tough.

Dan Rooney

Here was the old soldier, cast off and disgraced, coming in to lead men who didn't want to be led by him. Here was the marshal of the Old West, whipped down and a failure, coming in to clean up a new town that didn't want to be cleaned up. The situation was made to order for him. Readying his weapons— cajolery with some men, an iron hand and a whiplashing tongue with others— Bobby Layne accepted the challenge.

Booton Herndon
author,
on the celebrated ex-Detroit
Lions quarterback upon his
arrival in the Steel City for the
1958 season

We needed a leader before we were going anywhere. Bobby Layne is the greatest leader I've ever been associated with. He'll set the pace for the rest of our players.

Buddy Parker

FAST FACT: Layne took the Steelers' field generalship in 1958, guiding them to a 7–4–1 record, Pittsburgh's first winning season since 1949.

He asks you to do something and you go out and break your neck to do it.

John Nisby
guard (1957–61),
on Bobby Layne

Bobby Layne . . . with even a small potbelly to announce his age, still had to be counted with the most aggressive, the sharpest-eyed, the most fiercely competitive, and the most relentless in fledging his teammates and their ancestors with quill-sharp epithets when they failed to fulfill his hopes.

Robert Smith
author

What a general—the MacArthur of the National Football League.

Lou Creekmur

Detroit Lions Hall of Fame offensive tackle, on Bobby Layne

◇ ◇ ◇

Bobby Layne's concept of the breakfast of champions was a large measure of alcohol with a pinch of Wheaties on the side.

GAMEDAY
Issue 12, 2002

◇ ◇ ◇

Robert Lawrence Layne . . . was Gary Cooper in the showdown in *High Noon*; he was Buck Jones heading off rustlers at the pass; he was Sam Houston leading the charge at San Jacinto, and he was Davy Crockett and Jim Bowie defying Santa Anna as the Alamo crumbled.

Murray Olderman

author/sports journalist

When he went on the field, Bobby Layne was in charge. *In* charge. There was no question of that from the first minute.

Dan Rooney

◇ ◇ ◇

A wrathful competitor, a man impossible to scare.

Robert Smith
on Bobby Layne

◇ ◇ ◇

We had never had anybody like Bobby Layne. He was one hundred percent competitive. He would throw the ball early. He was a smart ballplayer. Win at all costs. There was no in between, no gray area. He played one way—all out.

Jack Butler

He was a Steeler's Steeler—tough, talented, and competitive, with a decided emphasis on tough.

Frank Lambert

punter (1965–66)/author,
on Bobby Layne

◇　◇　◇

There are many who claim Bobby Layne was the best quarterback who ever lived. It certainly would be difficult to name more than a few who were his equal.

Bob Collins

sportswriter

◇　◇　◇

His teammates said that while his passes were "ugly," they were accurate. He played the game hard and expected everybody else on the team to do the same, never shrinking from publicly beating those who missed assignments.

Frank Lambert

on Bobby Layne

John Henry Johnson was a great football player. He could do everything. He was tough, strong; he could run, block, catch. He did it all.

Jack Butler

on the future Hall of Fame running back who played with Pittsburgh from 1960 through 1965

John Henry plays mean, but not dirty. A lot of the guys play it rough, but they don't have that natural something—the timing or whatever it is—that John Henry has when he whips that shoulder into you.

Anonymous Steelers teammate

If I had to go into a dark alley, and I had my pick of one man to go with me, I'd want that man to be John Henry Johnson.

Anonymous Steelers lineman

They'll find out who he is.

Chuck Noll

*replying to critics of the Steelers'
1969 first-round pick, a no-name
defensive tackle out of North
Texas State named "Mean Joe"
Greene. The local press had
pouted, "Joe Who?"*

◇   ◇   ◇

He was unquestionably the player of
the decade. There was no player who
was more valuable to his team.

Andy Russell

on "Mean Joe" Greene

◇   ◇   ◇

Look around the league and you know
who the tough guys are, because they
developed that reputation. Joe Greene was
obviously one of those type guys, a tough
guy. If you look at teams that are successful, there's a bunch of guys there like that.

Gene Upshaw

*16-year Oakland Raiders Hall
of Fame guard/NFL Players
Association executive director*

AP / WIDE WORLD PHOTO

"Mean Joe" Greene

He was the best leader I've ever seen in my life.

Dan Rooney
on Joe Greene

◇ ◇ ◇

He picked up the "Mean" tag at North Texas State, where the team itself was called the Mean Green. In truth, he hated the nickname, and it took him years to make peace with it—and his image.

Abby Mendelson

◇ ◇ ◇

Joe brought everything. He had great physical skills, emotional intensity, and love for the game. He was an intelligent ballplayer, studying the game, doing the right things, and being prepared. Through his leadership he motivated the people around him to be better than they would normally have been.

Lynn Swann
on Joe Greene

I never saw him lose a battle.

Chuck Noll

on defensive tackle Joe Greene

◇   ◇   ◇

He was so quick, so strong, that offensive linemen couldn't block him. When he decided to come, it did not matter. People had never seen anything like Joe Greene.

Ralph Berlin

◇   ◇   ◇

Joe was the best defensive lineman I've ever seen.

Dick Hoak

◇   ◇   ◇

Joe Greene was what that team was built on; his fierceness, his competitiveness, and his never-say-die attitude. I never saw anybody who could block Joe in his first five years. I couldn't block Joe—and he didn't even go full speed in practice.

Ray Mansfield

Joe Greene did not know fear. One time he spit in Dick Butkus's face. Butkus had the presence of mind to walk away.

Ralph Berlin

◇ ◇ ◇

Joe Greene was the boss. Whenever I had a problem, I never went to Chuck Noll. I never went to Dan Rooney. I went to Joe.

Ralph Berlin

◇ ◇ ◇

There was never a player more loyal to his team than Joe Greene . . . there will never be another like him.

Art Rooney

◇ ◇ ◇

He's the most damaging big back I've seen.

Hank Stram
*Kansas City Chiefs Hall of Fame
head coach,
on Franco Harris*

The fun of running was reading, vision, and doing what I had to do at that time—making something happen to make the team successful. I always looked for something big. Make the big play.

Franco Harris

He had the arm to throw soap bubbles through a telephone pole.

Gerry Dulac

on Terry Bradshaw

The quarterback is normally the guy you look at, the guy who will bring 'em back. Joe Namath was like that. So was Terry Bradshaw. All the good ones. You always knew there were guys like that who could beat you anytime—first quarter, fifth quarter, didn't matter.

Gene Upshaw

He was as good a football player as I've ever seen in my life. And he may have been Noll's best effort. Chuck handled Terry Bradshaw perfectly.

Dan Rooney

◇ ◇ ◇

Chuck recognized my strengths— strong arm, impatient, hated short passes, loved to challenge safeties and corners as opposed to linebackers—and put this offense in for me. It wasn't a West Coast offense. It was one pass, from East Coast to West Coast. It was fun.

Terry Bradshaw

◇ ◇ ◇

The only reason I got into the Hall of Fame is because of my rings. You can't look at my statistics and say, "Those are Hall of Fame statistics." It's always been about the rings.

Terry Bradshaw

AP / WIDE WORLD PHOTO

Terry Bradshaw

We ain't gonna lose when he's hot.

Joe Greene

on Terry Bradshaw

◇ ◇ ◇

He's the kind of guy who could excel at anything, at any position. I think he could make it as a tight end, a linebacker, you name it. Even as a runner. He and Mike Kruczek would punt back and forth with each other across the field, and Terry would consistently punt the ball fifty or fifty-five yards with great accuracy.

Joe Gordon

former director of public relations, on Terry Bradshaw

Lynn Swann was a performing artist whose stage was a football field. His weekly Sunday recitals were showstoppers that left audiences awestruck. His leaping fingertip catches were made with the grace of a ballet dancer. His pass patterns across the middle were run with the fearlessness of a circus high-wire walker. And, like other great entertainers, his finest performances often came in the final act, when it meant the most.

Joe Horrigan

Pro Football Hall of Fame
vice president of communications/
exhibits

◇   ◇   ◇

I'd like to say that we developed Lynn Swann. But the truth is he was perfectly developed as a football player the first time he stepped on our practice field.

Chuck Noll

◇   ◇   ◇

Big plays are not called to be a big play. They're just called.

Lynn Swann

His big thing was his great timing and his ability to jump. His timing was phenomenal. He knew when to go up. Great hands, great eye-hand coordination. He was a tough little guy and took a lot of big hits.

Jack Butler

on Lynn Swann

When John Stallworth and I arrived we became dangerous throwing the football—we could beat teams throwing the football. John and I established a reputation that if we put the ball in the air we could hurt you very badly with only three to five catches in the ballgame. But it wasn't something we lived off.

Lynn Swann

◇ ◇ ◇

Swann got all the ink, Stallworth wound up with the numbers.

Abby Mendelson

He's great. He's a Hall of Famer, or should be. He's competitive. He competes on every play. He never quits. If he's close to the ball, you know he's going to catch it. He didn't get to the Super Bowl four times for nothing. I've always said that John Stallworth is a better receiver than Lynn Swann.

Ronnie Lott
San Francisco 49ers Hall of Fame strong safety,
1984

◇ ◇ ◇

Mike Webster was a tough guy who'd tape up his jersey sleeves to intimidate the other team.

Dan Rooney

◇ ◇ ◇

As one veteran writer put it, "nothing short of an Act of Congress" would keep Mike Webster from taking his place in the Steelers starting lineup.

Joe Horrigan

In the final game of the 1975 season, Steelers coach Chuck Noll decided to insert Mike Webster into the starting lineup. It was the beginning of a remarkable string of 150 consecutive starts that lasted until 1986, when he missed the first four games with a dislocated elbow. . . . Those were the only games "Iron Mike" would miss during his first 16 seasons.

Joe Horrigan

That's the toughness I like. Not a macho toughness, where you've got to strut it around, but an inner toughness, the John Wayne type who doesn't complain.

Ray Mansfield
on his onetime understudy, future Hall of Fame center Mike Webster

Webster lifted weights in his hospital bed.

George Perles

John Wayne may have been fiction in heroics. Mike's not fiction. Mike's real.

Chuck Noll

on nine-time Pro Bowler Mike Webster

Nobody could outwork Mike. Physically, there were others who were taller, bigger, and stronger. But he was a good student, a tough guy who wanted to play. He also played with a fear of not being good or not being successful at what he did.

Larry Brown

tight end/offensive tackle (1971–84), on Mike Webster

You have to be so demanding of yourself. Because those aren't the Boy Scouts out there. It's a dangerous place.

Mike Webster

Webster was flat-out the best. He knew what everybody was doing. He made all the line calls. Sometimes we'd be in a play, and the quarterback would be in a cadence, and Webbie would look back and say, "Get out of it," and they respected Webster so much they would change.

Tunch Ilkin

After 15 years, I don't care how tired he was, he ran up to the ball. He always gave 100 percent, no matter what. I try to do the same.

Dermontti Dawson
*center (1988–2000),
on his predecessor, "Iron Mike"
Webster*

Lambert, he's bizarre, he's wild.

J. T. Thomas

Jack Lambert may have had the image of a wild man, but he killed you with his precision. He was a great anticipator. Read his keys. Penetrator. Took angles away from blockers. Great technique. Never made a mistake. But what really sets him aside as a great middle linebacker was his ability to cover the pass—he was dramatically better than anyone on the pass. He covered the tight end man-for-man. He covered the first back out—that's unheard of. Lambert did things never asked of a middle linebacker—and did them superbly.

Andy Russell

He's so mean he hates himself.

J. T. Thomas
on Lambert

Jack Lambert. I think that guy was a smart guy. His whole image was a tough guy, but he was smarter—he was "playing" that.

Joe DeLamielleure
*Buffalo Bills/Cleveland Browns
Hall of Fame guard*

◇ ◇ ◇

No question, people don't recognize that Jack, as a rookie, which was our first Super Bowl year (1974), was a middle linebacker making all the calls, making all the calls for the defensive fronts as well as all the secondary calls, as a rookie. That's a very difficult job to do. I concur with Joe DeLamielleure. Lambert was a very, very bright guy. Smart guy.

Jack Ham

◇ ◇ ◇

The stunt 4–3 freed Jack Lambert up, allowing him to play his game, to take advantage of his natural talents. The stunt 4–3 and the double zone turned Pittsburgh from a loser into a winner.

Bud Carson
assistant coach (1972–77)

I really would've liked to have played in the 1950s and '60s when men were men. They talk about how rough the game is today, how big and strong they are, but if you watch games from the '50s and '60s, every time a quarterback goes back to pass, there was roughing the passer. They were clotheslining people, and there was no foul.

Jack Lambert
middle linebacker (1974–84)

We were in sync, like a symphony. We enjoyed being with each other. On the football field we were friends. We just blended together.

L. C. Greenwood
on the Steel Curtain's legendary front four

Andy Russell, Jack Ham, and Jack Lambert—our linebackers were all 220 pounds, ran 4.5 forties, and were smart as all get-out. Those are the kind of people Chuck Noll wanted. Because smart people don't make mistakes.

Terry Bradshaw

I just play emotionally. Jack Ham plays and never says a word. I yell and scream a lot.

Jack Lambert

He's the best I ever saw for coverage. There was nobody like him.

Bud Carson
on Jack Ham

During one playoff game in Pittsburgh, we ran a screen pass. Jack Ham didn't see me, but I saw him. I hit him right in his thigh; it was a really good, clean shot, but a hard shot. I thought to myself, 'Well, that's it for him for the day.' He went out for one play and he was back. When you talk about the Steelers in those days, everybody was like that.

Gene Upshaw

My biggest strength was one-on-one, man-to-man coverage. I had an advantage with my height and very long arms. I could be beat, but I could cover so well because my arms are long. It worked out.

Mel Blount

Jerome Bettis

I made a living on carrying people. That's why they call me "The Bus."

Jerome Bettis

running back (1996–2005)

◇   ◇   ◇

Jerome is in a class by himself.

Shaun Alexander

*Seattle Seahawks running back
and the NFL's 2005 MVP,
on The Bus*

6

LEGENDARY COACHES

Chuck was the best nonverbal communicator in the world. He had a way of telling you that you were the best—or that you would not be here next year—just with a look. If you weren't into nonverbal communication, you missed Chuck Noll.

J. T. Thomas

John fit right in with our team. He didn't believe in fundamentals.

Art Rooney

on head coach Johnny "Blood" McNally, the Hall of Fame halfback who played and coached the Steelers from 1937 through '39

He was not only one of the game's great players, but also one of its great personalities, a bon vivant whose lifestyle was ideally suited to "The Roaring Twenties." Long before hell-raising Paul Hornung came to Green Bay, Johnny Blood was tearing up the town—and any other he happened to be in. Red Smith, the late great sports columnist, called him "unfettered," as good an adjective as any to describe Blood's aversion to convention.

Dan Daly

writer/author

He could be with the riff-raff on the waterfront one night, then recite Keats and Shelley or Shakespeare by the hour in elite company the next.

Ollie Kuechle

1930s Milwaukee Journal
sportswriter,
on the ubiquitous Johnny "Blood" McNally

On most other teams, the coaches worry about the players showing up for practice or missing bed check. With us, the players worry about the coach.

Art Rooney

on good-timing Johnny "Blood" McNally

John was a good teammate, a cheerful fellow, friendly off the field. Nothing fazed him. Sometimes, although he was a player-coach, he might miss a practice and explain the next day that he had been to the library.

Byron "Whizzer" White

on Johnny "Blood" McNally

As a head coach, Johnny Blood made a terrific halfback.

Abby Mendelson

> *FAST FACT*: Blood, a future Hall of Famer as the NFL's first great pass-catching halfback, coached the Pittsburgh Pirates for nearly three full seasons (1937–39), often playing halfback as well.

I had no ambition to coach. I didn't cotton to the idea. It wasn't that I had any fears about being able to coach successfully. I knew I had the brains because it doesn't take much brains to be a coach. Character is more important.

Johnny "Blood" McNally

who coached the Pirates to a 6–19 record during his three seasons at the Pittsburgh helm

Too dumb. The kid was just too dumb to be a pro quarterback.

Walt Kiesling
guard-tackle (1937–38)/assistant coach (1938–39, 1941, 1949–54, 1957–61)/head coach (1939–40, 1941–44, 1954–56),
asked by a Steelers executive why he had cut ninth-round draftee Johnny Unitas after three weeks of summer camp in 1955

Walt Kiesling took multiple turns as head coach. From all accounts he was a decent football man with all of the smarts—but none of the temperament to make much of a difference. Overall, his record was a sorry 30–55–5.

Abby Mendelson

Dr. John Bain "Jock" Sutherland was a man born to be either a Scottish chieftain or a football coach. A dentist hailing from the old country, he was a fabled Pitt player and coach. Bringing him in was nothing short of The Chief's biggest public relations coup since signing Whizzer White in 1938.

Abby Mendelson

on the onetime Steelers head coach

This was a professional coach: scientific, precise, and demanding. Like Chuck Noll twenty years later, Jock Sutherland had a system, a vision for what he wanted. The Steelers had never seen anything like it.

Abby Mendelson

on the Steelers coach of the mid-1940s

For the two years Jock Sutherland coached, 1946–47, Forbes Field was sold out and the Steelers actually won more than they lost. Ultimately, his untimely post-season death from a brain tumor robbed the club of its first great coach.

Abby Mendelson

Raymond "Buddy" Parker joined the elite club of Chuck Noll, Bill Cowher, and Jock Sutherland as one of only four coaches ever to compile a winning record with the Steelers, 51–48–6.

Abby Mendelson
on the Pittsburgh head coach
from 1957 through '64

I interviewed Chuck Noll the day after his team, the Baltimore Colts, lost Super Bowl III to the New York Jets. It struck me right then. Here is an extremely bright person who has his feet on the ground, knows what he is doing.

Dan Rooney

Chuck Noll knew what he wanted to do. He knew the type of player he wanted. He wasn't just going out and getting players to fill in for a year or two. He knew he wanted to build a team through the draft. He wanted guys who understood the game. He had a plan. You could see it.

Dick Hoak

Chuck Noll really had brass balls. Once he told me that's what was needed to run a successful football team. There wasn't a bit of phony in him. The Rooneys were all people people. Noll was like General George Marshall, and that was just what we needed.

Art Rooney Jr.

◇ ◇ ◇

He wanted things taught, and he wanted them taught his way because it was almost impossible to find a coach who knew as much about offense and defense as Chuck Noll did. He had a background that was second to none.

George Perles

FAST FACT: Noll apprenticed as an assistant under Sid Gillman at San Diego and with Don Shula at Baltimore before taking the head coaching job at Pittsburgh in 1969.

It's better to give than to receive. It's better to hit than to be hit.

Chuck Noll

◇ ◇ ◇

He was very methodical. Very well thought out in everything he said. He never said anything off the cuff. He never said anything in anger.

Ray Mansfield
on Chuck Noll

◇ ◇ ◇

I had been associated with championship teams in Cleveland, Los Angeles, San Diego, and Baltimore. So the stuff that I believed in had been successful in a lot of places. It was all good stuff—and you don't change it overnight. It was just a question of execution. You have to have people to do that, and that takes some time.

Chuck Noll

Noll was an individual who really had it. He ruled with an iron hand. "This is the way we do things. If you don't like it, you find some other place to do it." You did it his way or there was no other way.

Jack Butler

Chuck Noll made one speech before every game. He made the same speech for the Super Bowl as he gave before the first preseason game. It was a business speech. "You've got this job to do," Chuck'd say. He never said, "Let's win this one for Mr. Rooney," or "Let's win it for the city of Pittsburgh." It was "Play for yourself and have fun."

Ralph Berlin

I have the utmost respect for Chuck Noll. The job of a coach is to push players. Chuck was able to do three things— bring talent, put it together in a package, and let everybody play football. And it worked. It absolutely worked.

Mike Wagner
safety (1971–80)

He was very even-keeled. If you had a bad game, he wasn't in your face. If you had a good game, he never said you were the world's greatest. I always enjoyed that about him, that quiet and confident understanding. He respected and admired the job I did.

Gary Anderson
on Chuck Noll

He put the muzzle on after the game and took it off at one o'clock the next week.

Dwight White

on Chuck Noll

I swear, Chuck sees everything that's going on with 22 men on the field. He's got the lousiest seat on the field, but there's nothing he doesn't see. He doesn't miss a trick. I have all kinds of trouble watching my people on the offensive line, but he sees the linemen, the quarterback, the receivers, and the defense all at the same time. It's incredible. It's just not real.

Rollie Dotsch

offensive line coach (1978–81)

He wouldn't let us feel too good about ourselves or feel too bad about ourselves.

Joe Greene

on Chuck Noll

He called upon you to look inside yourself and see what you want to be and how you want to prepare yourself. It runs through Chuck Noll's career: If a team is prepared they can beat a team that is not prepared.

Ray Mansfield

◇ ◇ ◇

Vince Lombardi with couth.

Phil Musick
on Chuck Noll

◇ ◇ ◇

Chuck Noll is an amazing man. Just having him on the sidelines is the equivalent of having an extra man on the field.

Rollie Dotsch

◇ ◇ ◇

"Whatever it takes" is an attitude. What we were trying to pass on is a winning attitude.

Chuck Noll

The most important thing as a player is to concentrate on progressing as a player and everything else will fall into place. Concentrate on winning and doing your job.

Chuck Noll

1989 may have been Chuck Noll's best year. He orchestrated one of the greatest turnarounds in club history. After the two most humiliating losses in Steeler history—a 51–0 drubbing by the Browns and a 41–10 disaster in Cincinnati—Noll never let the team panic. Rallying his troops and redirecting them, he piloted the club to a 9–7 finish, returning to the playoffs for the first time in five years.

Abby Mendelson

You can talk to Bill [Cowher]. Chuck [Noll] didn't do that. If he had something to say to you, he'd call you in and talk to you. He wasn't going to invite you to dinner at his house. Chuck's door was always open, but you wouldn't go in to talk to Chuck about some things. Bill's more like one of the guys.

Dick Hoak

◇   ◇   ◇

He made a system fit the players instead of making the players fit the system. When Coach Cowher did that, he provided the opportunity for the players to blossom.

Rod Woodson

◇   ◇   ◇

Coach Cowher is very intense. Yet you can still talk to him. Off the field, he cares about you.

Ernie Mills
wide receiver (1991–96)

Coach Cowher's done an outstanding job. He inherited a team that had a lot of talent, and he molded that talent into his own team. Everybody says he's a player's coach—because he talks to players and has an open line of communication. He also respects every player on the football team and gives each one an opportunity to prove himself. They play a lot harder for themselves and the team.

Rod Woodson

There was no doubt that he's one of us. There was no question that he was going to fit in. He was almost an extension of Chuck Noll. He's a Pittsburgher.

Dan Rooney
on Bill Cowher

Marty Schottenheimer is the backbone of my coaching career. He taught me the importance of being organized. Practices. What and how you present to the players. Dealing with each person, in adversity and success. He taught me to be consistent but demanding; to motivate players and get the most out of them.

Bill Cowher

◇ ◇ ◇

In this business you have to be able to make decisions. You can't let your heart overcome what you need to do.

Bill Cowher

◇ ◇ ◇

His personality sold me on the team. Basically, I said I really want to play for this guy.

Kevin Greene
*linebacker (1993–95),
on Bill Cowher*

As a marginal player you've got to find the way to succeed. So you'll spend the extra time studying, working, or trying to find that little edge that'll get you up to the gifted guy. The work ethic that you bring to the game as a marginal athlete is one that you can take over into coaching.

Bill Cowher

a self-described "marginal athlete" as a five-year NFL special teams player with Cleveland and Philadelphia

◇ ◇ ◇

If you stay at things and don't ever stop believing, you make your own good fortune.

Bill Cowher

◇ ◇ ◇

No one could ever forget Chuck Noll's steely eyed, thin-lipped fury or Bill Cowher's Wagnerian outbursts—fuel that powered the club.

Abby Mendelson

When it's time to be playful, he'll joke with the players. . . . But when it's time to get on the field and get better, he's all business, baby. You respect that. It makes you want to go out and fight even harder for the guy.

Hines Ward
on Bill Cowher

The only thing that has been missing on his résumé is a championship. Now he has that championship. I think you have to consider him one of the best coaches in the game.

Jerome Bettis
*on Bill Cowher, following
Super Bowl XL*

MAJOR MOMENTS

7

The Immaculate Reception was the one play that changed our belief system, the one play that became a stepping stone to greatness, the one play that led us to four Super Bowls.

Rocky Bleier

There you go, boys. That's the way it should be done.

Johnny "Blood" McNally

to fellow Pirate players following his 100-yard opening kickoff return for a touchdown against Philadelphia in his first game as Pittsburgh's player-head coach, in 1937. The Pirates beat the Eagles, 27–14

Joe Geri's three-year career (1949–51) included the longest punt in Steeler history, 82 yards, on October 20, 1949, versus the Green Bay Packers.

Abby Mendelson

Can you help us, son?

John Michelosen

*head coach (1948–51),
to young quarterback Jim Finks
at halftime of a 1951 game
against Washington, with
Pittsburgh down, 10–0. Finks,
a defensive back, responded,
guiding the Steelers to three
second-half touchdowns and a
20–10 victory. Finks became
Pittsburgh's regular quarterback
for the next four years*

Lynn Chandnois had a big day that day. He ran back one kick for a touchdown and ran for another touchdown.

George Hughes

*on the 63–7 obliteration of the
New York Giants, November 30,
1952, the most points scored by
a Steelers team to that time and
the worst defeat ever suffered by
the Giants. Pittsburgh held New
York to just 15 yards rushing*

Now I know how those people in Hiroshima felt.

Harry Wismer
former New York Giants broadcaster, following the 3–6 Steelers' 63–7 demolition of the Giants in 1952 at Forbes Field. Quarterback Jim Finks bombed New York for 254 yards passing and four touchdowns

The Steelers rolled up 683 yards on an icy, slippery, gridiron that would have been more appropriate for the Ice Capades. Only one other pro team ever exceeded the Steelers' offensive output yesterday—the Los Angeles Rams, who in 1951 overwhelmed the New York Yanks with a total of 735 yards.

Pat Livingston
Pittsburgh writer/author

FAST FACT: Pittsburgh quarterback Bobby Layne tossed a Steelers-record 409 yards passing, while receiver Jimmy Orr pulled in six passes for 205 yards and three touchdowns, including strikes of 86 and 72 yards. Defensive back Dean Derby picked off three Chicago Cardinals aerials in the 38–21 rout at Pitt Stadium, December 13, 1958.

I have no doubt we would have beaten the Giants with Layne at quarterback that day. Ed Brown was never the leader Layne was, and that's what we needed that day—a leader.

Buddy Parker

after the 33–17 loss to New York at Yankee Stadium, December 15, 1963. A win that afternoon would have given the Steelers the Eastern Division crown and their first-ever title in franchise history

John Henry Johnson, barging over the goal line on runs of 33, 45, and 5 yards, set a personal high of 200 yards on 30 carries—a club record that put Johnson into the exclusive 200-yards-in-one-game club.

Pat Livingston

on the Hall of Fame fullback's big day in Pittsburgh's 23–7 win over Cleveland, October 10, 1964

We had to have that game in Houston to win the division. And we were having a tough time. The offense failed to convert, and as the defense went back on the field, defensive back John Rowser said, "Damn it, here we go again." Joe Greene said, "I'll be damned if we are." And he sacked Dan Pastorini four straight downs.

Ralph Berlin

FAST FACT: Pittsburgh went on to win that December 10, 1972, game, 9–3.

◇ ◇ ◇

The National Football League's Little Boy Lost has been found . . . 40 years of gloom drowned in a champagne bottle.

Phil Musick

his Pittsburgh Press *lead,*
December 18, 1972, the day after
the Steelers' 24–2 win over
San Diego gave Pittsburgh the
AFC Central Division crown—
its first-ever title

Up until that point, I was the one who was believing that this was a good football team. This was a sign that this was a team of destiny.

Chuck Noll

on the era-altering Immaculate Reception

That afternoon we discovered we could play with anybody.

Joe Greene

in the aftermath of the phenomenal 13–7 AFC playoff victory over Oakland, December 23, 1972—the Steelers' first playoff game ever, topped by Franco Harris's impeccable Immaculate Reception

We hadn't had anything like that happen to us in our history, and in my lifetime. It was a special moment. People there didn't believe what they saw happened.

Art Rooney II

Steelers president (2003–),
who witnessed the Immaculate
Reception as a Steelers ball boy
in '72

I learned early at Penn State to always be around the ball, be around the action. Maybe there'll be a fumble. Maybe I'll throw a block. Because of that attitude the Immaculate Reception happened.

Franco Harris

the all-time club leader in
touchdowns (100) and yards
rushing (11,950)

AP / WIDE WORLD PHOTO

Franco Harris legs it out after making the Immaculate Reception.

I was standing near the end zone watching the game wind down. I saw Bradshaw throw the pass and the ball bounce off Frenchy Fuqua. Suddenly Franco came out of nowhere to catch the ball. He ran down the sidelines straight at me. I began yelling, "Come on, Franco. Come on. You can make it." You can see me on the film replays jumping around and waving my arms to urge Franco on. I'm the little guy in the trench coat with my back turned to the camera. I've watched a lot of games in my time. I saw plenty of big plays. But the Immaculate Reception remains the greatest moment of my career. It's at the top of my list.

Myron Cope

The Immaculate Reception. . . . Every time I come to the stadium, I walk in there and my son [John Jr.] asks, "Hey, Dad, is that where Tatum knocked your head off?"

John "Frenchy" Fuqua
running back (1970–76)

◇   ◇   ◇

Franco had been blocking on the play and then went out. He was hustling . . . and all good things happen to those who keep hustling.

Chuck Noll

◇   ◇   ◇

I knew the ball would bounce that way.

Franco Harris
on Terry Bradshaw's caromed pass in the 1972 AFC playoff game with Oakland that bounced off running back Frenchy Fuqua and Raiders safety Jack Tatum to Harris. The future Hall of Fame running back's shoe-top catch and resulting touchdown run instantly entered NFL folklore as the Immaculate Reception

I've played football since the second grade. Nothing like that ever happened. It'll never happen again.

Terry Bradshaw
on the Immaculate Reception

To this day, no single event, not even Bill Mazeroski's home run in the 1960 World Series, generates more goose bumps among the Pittsburgh sporting faithful than Franco's Immaculate Reception.

Gerry Dulac

After 40 endless years of spilling salt and breaking mirrors and walking under ladders, the Steelers were smiled upon by a benevolent fate.

Phil Musick
on Franco Harris's Immaculate Reception

When we won the first Super Bowl, none of Mr. Rooney's sons came into the locker room. They stayed out on purpose, because this was The Chief's day. The players hollered, "Chief! Chief! Chief!" and gave him the game ball. Then NFL Commissioner Pete Rozelle presented to him the Super Bowl trophy. There wasn't a dry eye in the place. Only after that did Dan and Art come in— that's the tremendous respect they had for their dad.

Ralph Berlin

I bet The Burg looks like Hiroshima.

Jim Clack
*center/guard (1971–77),
to Ray Mansfield, following the
Steelers' 16–6 triumph over
Minnesota in Super Bowl IX,
their first-ever Super Bowl win*

We had the desire and the will to win the biggest game in the history of the Steelers up to that time. I'm not underestimating the talent, but our attitude was so high. The zone is not a place that you visit very often. You're lucky if you get there once in your career. That's where we were that day as a team.

Joe Greene

on Pittsburgh's 24–13 victory in the 1974 AFC Championship Game at Oakland

That game showed the true essence of the Steelers. It made us believe we were a great football team. From that moment on, we had the feeling that we were going to win.

Franco Harris

on the 1974 AFC title game win over the Raiders

Who could ever forget Jack Lambert defending Steeler kicker Roy Gerela by body slamming Dallas Cowboy safety Cliff Harris in Super Bowl X?

Austin Murphy

FAST FACT: Gerela had missed a field goal attempt and was taunted by Harris who patted the dejected kicker on the back, prompting Lambert's outburst.

◇ ◇ ◇

I felt it was uncalled for, and someone had to do something about it. . . . I don't like the idea of people slapping our kicker or jumping up in his face and laughing when he misses a field goal.

Jack Lambert

on his infamous Super Bowl X retaliation of Dallas Cowboys safety Cliff Harris's taunt of Roy Gerela, following the kicker's second missed field goal try

Three of his catches, as one veteran reporter noted, were of the "break-out-the-thesaurus variety."

Joe Horrigan

on Lynn Swann's Super Bowl X MVP performance: four catches for 161 yards, setting up one touchdown and tallying the game-winner against Dallas on a 64-yard scoring reception. In between, Swann recorded a 53-yard circus catch, tipping the ball in mid air, twisting, then finally catching the ball while on the ground

When he broke free, I thought it was a touchdown. I just said, "Get 'em towel."

Mike Wagner

on the legendary Super Bowl XIII-turning drop of a third-quarter Roger Staubach touchdown pass by Dallas tight end Jackie Smith, wide open in the Steelers' end zone. A catch by Smith would have tied the game at 21–all

I think the Steelers and Cowboys have played the two most exciting games ever to be played in the Super Bowl.

Rocky Bleier

his reference to Pittsburgh's 21–17 and 35–31 triumphs over Dallas in Super Bowls X and XIII respectively

This is my most satisfying Super Bowl ever. I felt more pressure than in any previous year because we were playing in L.A., and we had never beaten the Rams. This is our fourth Super Bowl title, and our team realized it was on the verge of setting history.

Terry Bradshaw

who collected his second consecutive Super Bowl MVP trophy following the Steelers' 31–19 victory over the Rams in Super Bowl XIV

If there's any one team that can win three in a row, we can do it.

Terry Bradshaw

after Pittsburgh had won its second consecutive Super Bowl and fourth in sixth years, with its defeat of Los Angeles, 31–19, in Super Bowl XIV

We weren't just beaten, we were embarrassed.

Mark Gastineau

former New York Jets defensive end, after his Jets were buried by the Steelers, 34–7, in early December 1983. The win clinched a wild-card playoff berth for Pittsburgh

◇ ◇ ◇

Indianapolis receivers and Steelers defensive backs packed into the end zone like bachelors waiting for the garter toss. The stakes: a trip to the Super Bowl.

Ed Bouchette

on the final play of the 1995 AFC Championship Game: Colts quarterback Jim Harbaugh's desperation Hail Mary pass into the Pittsburgh end zone that narrowly missed being caught for a touchdown. The Steelers stole a 20–16 victory and headed to Super Bowl XXX

I'll always remember Super Bowl XXX. Even though we lost to the Cowboys [27–17], we were in it to the end.

Bill Cowher

Once in a blue moon, Jerome fumbles. Once in a blue moon, I make a tackle. They just happened to be in the same game.

Ben Roethlisberger

on his game- and season-saving open-field tackle of Indianapolis cornerback Nick Harper's return of Jerome Bettis's popup fumble on the Indy 2-yard line late in the Steelers' 21–18 win over the Colts in the 2005 AFC divisional playoffs. Harper appeared to have clear sailing ahead after picking up the fumble, but Roethlisberger's athletic tackle kept alive Bettis's dream of returning to his hometown of Detroit for Super Bowl XL

Roethlisberger had vowed to Jerome Bettis early in the 2005 season that he would reward the veteran running back for delaying his retirement for a year, by guiding the Steelers to a Super Bowl berth in Detroit, the future Hall of Fame runner's hometown. He delivered on that promise in huge fashion as the Steelers defeated each of the top three seeds in the conference, all on the road.

Len Pasquarelli

ESPN.com

FAST FACT: In the Steelers' three 2005 postseason victories leading up to Super Bowl XL, Big Ben threw seven touchdown passes, just one interception, and logged a 124.4 passer efficiency rating.

*Hines Ward scores after snagging a toss from
Randle El in Super Bowl XL*

AP / WIDE WORLD PHOTO

They called a great play at the right time. The offensive line did a heck of a job and Antwaan did a heck of a job.

Hines Ward
whose 43-yard fourth-quarter touchdown reception from Antwaan Randle El off a reverse pass produced the final Steelers touchdown in the 21–10 Super Bowl XL win over Seattle

It's one thing to throw a touchdown in the regular season, but the Super Bowl? Wow. Wow!

Antwaan Randle El
wide receiver (2002–05), on his 43-yard scoring toss to Hines Ward to climax the Super Bowl XL victory

If you look at the history of the Pittsburgh Steelers, people talk about Lynn Swann and John Stallworth making spectacular plays in the Super Bowl. I never felt I belonged with those guys. Now, I do.

Hines Ward

following his two-touchdown Super Bowl XL performance and selection as MVP

Mr. Rooney, I've been waiting a long time to do this. This is yours, man.

Bill Cowher

handing the Vince Lombardi Trophy to Steelers chairman Dan Rooney following Pittsburgh's 21–10 victory over Seattle in Super Bowl XL

THE PITTSBURGH STEELERS ALL-TIME TEAM

Johnny Blood, Whizzer White, Jim Finks, Lynn Chandnois, Ray Mathews, Bobby Layne, John Henry Johnson, Lynn Swann, Dwight White, Greg Lloyd, Jerome Bettis . . . and those are just some of the stars who didn't *make it!*

Most are unrivaled icons—Bradshaw, quarterback; Harris, running back; Greene, defensive tackle. Even leaving earlier-era Elbie Nickel as an end rather than conforming him into either a wideout or a tight end seems reasonable in this idyllic gathering of greats.

There would be little argument that cornerback/ returner Rod Woodson is the finest athlete ever to don a Steelers uniform; therefore, it's not surprising that he makes the all-time team at two positions.

Forthwith, the Pittsburgh Steelers All-Time Team:

PITTSBURGH STEELERS ALL-TIME TEAM

OFFENSE
John Stallworth, *wide receiver*
Jon Kolb, *tackle*
Alan Faneca, *guard*
Mike Webster, center
Sam Davis, *guard*
Frank Varrichione, *tackle*
Elbie Nickel, *end*
Hines Ward, *wide receiver*
Terry Bradshaw, *quarterback*
Franco Harris, *running back*
"Bullet Bill" Dudley, *running back*

DEFENSE
L. C. Greenwood, *defensive end*
"Mean Joe" Greene, *defensive tackle*
Ernie Stautner, *defensive tackle*
Bill McPeak, *defensive end*
Jack Ham, *linebacker*
Jack Lambert, *middle linebacker*
Andy Russell, *linebacker*
Mel Blount, *cornerback*
Jack Butler, *free safety*
Donnie Shell, *strong safety*
Rod Woodson, *cornerback*

SPECIALISTS
Pat Brady, *punter*
Gary Anderson, *kicker*
Rod Woodson, *punt returner*
Lynn Chandnois, *kick returner*

Chuck Noll, *head coach*

JOHN STALLWORTH

Wide Receiver (1974–87)

Pro Bowls (4), All-Pro (1979),
Steelers MVP (1979, 1984),
Pro Football Hall of Fame (2002)

He is regarded as one of the most prolific performers in playoff history, having caught 12 touchdowns in postseason play, second all-time to Jerry Rice. He stands No. 1 all time in playoff history for most consecutive games with a touchdown reception (eight) and still holds two Super Bowl records outright: highest average gain, career (24.4 yards per catch) and highest average gain, game (40.33, Super Bowl XIV).

Lindy's 2002 Pro Football
on John Stallworth

JON KOLB
Tackle (1969–81)
All-AFC (1975, 1978)

It was the Jon Kolbs that made the great teams of the seventies go. . . . The toughest defensive ends—Jim Marshall, Harvey Martin (twice), and Fred Dryer—never touched Terry Bradshaw even once in the four Super Bowls.

Robert Oates Jr.
author

ALAN FANECA
Guard (1998–)
Pro Bowls (5)

Former number-one draft pick has developed into an All-Pro performer for the Steelers since being inserted into the starting lineup . . . earned his fifth consecutive trip to the Pro Bowl in 2006 . . . earned All-Pro honors by The Associated Press and *The Sporting News* in 2004 and was a selection to *Pro Football Weekly*'s All-NFL team that same year.

Steelers.com

MIKE WEBSTER
Center (1974–88)
Pro Bowls (9),
Pro Football Hall of Fame (1997)

Watch any other lineman in the league; they all saunter up to the line. But Mike sprints to the line on every play. That's intimidating. He whipped your butt on the last play and here he comes sprinting up to do it again.

Bill Meyers
*assistant coach (1984),
on Webster, the Steelers offensive
captain for nine seasons*

Every offensive lineman wants to grow up to be Mike Webster. But when God made him, he used a different kind of material. There will never be another one like him.

Craig Wolfley
guard/tackle (1980–89)

SAM DAVIS
Guard (1967–79)

Though he never made the Pro Bowl, Sam Davis is regarded as the best guard in Steelers history.

Ed Bouchette

1994

FRANK VARRICHIONE
Tackle (1955–60)
Pro Bowls (5)

In all the years Frank played for the Steelers, he was very seldom beaten outright. He had the respect of all the defensive linemen who played against him.

Ernie Stautner

on Varrichione

ELBIE NICKEL
End (1947–57)
Pro Bowls (3)

Nickel was neither a wide receiver nor a tight end, simply an end, in those days when receivers were not further delineated by position. Nickel was a three-time selectee to the Pro Bowl (1952, '53, '56) and led the NFL in average yards per catch (24.3) in 1949. He was the franchise's leading all-time receiver in catches and receiving yards before future Hall of Famers Lynn Swann and John Stallworth collected both marks in the late seventies. Big enough to block and rugged enough to catch in a crowd, Nickel was called "fast and tricky and a classy pass snagger" by a Steelers Web site in the UK.

HINES WARD

Wide Receiver (1998–),

Pro Bowls (4), Steelers MVP (2003),
Super Bowl XL MVP (2005),
Steelers all-time leader in receptions

Hines is like a pit bull. If he latches on to you, it's over. It's his makeup.

Kenny Jackson

former Steelers receiving coach, on Ward's blocking

◇　◇　◇

We can't win without him.

Joey Porter

on Ward

◇　◇　◇

I'm going to Disney World! And I'm taking "The Bus"!

Hines Ward

following his selection as Super Bowl XL MVP

TERRY BRADSHAW

Quarterback (1970–83)

Pro Bowls (3), NFL MVP (1978),
Steelers MVP (1977–78), All-Pro (1978),
Super Bowl XIII-XIV MVP,
Pro Football Hall of Fame (1989)

Jack Butler told me that there wouldn't be another player like Terry Bradshaw around for 10 or more years. I felt the same way.

Art Rooney Jr.

Terry Bradshaw had more talent at his position than anybody I'd ever seen.

Dick Hoak

FRANCO HARRIS

Running Back (1972–83)

Pro Bowls (8), All-Pro (1977),
Super Bowl IX MVP,
NFL Rookie of the Year (1972),
Pro Football Hall of Fame (1990)

He was the soul of the team.

Dan Rooney

on Franco Harris

There were a lot of good players on that team. But to me the single most important guy, the big money player, the guy who'd get you the tough first down, the guy who kept the ball when you needed to keep it, the guy the team rallied around, was Franco Harris.

Joe Greene

"Bullet Bill" Dudley

Running Back (1942, 1945–46)

Pro Bowls (3), All-Pro (1942, '46),
NFL MVP (1946),
Pro Football Hall of Fame (1966)

Bullet Bill Dudley, Art Rooney always said, was the finest player he'd ever had.

Andrew O'Toole

Bill Dudley ran like he was staggering, threw the ball like it was a loaf of bread, and kicked it clumsier than anybody I've ever seen. All he could do was beat you.

Paul Christman
*former Chicago Cardinals
quarterback*

L. C. GREENWOOD
Defensive End (1969–81)
Pro Bowls (6),
All-Pro (1974–75)

While his teammates wore the uniform's black shoes, Greenwood's shoes always were gold. In 1971, he combined with Joe Greene to form a nearly impregnable left side of the Steelers' defensive line. A nightmare for quarterbacks, Greenwood used his 6–6 height and quick reflexes to bat down numerous passes. In Super Bowl IX, he swatted three of Fran Tarkenton's attempts; when the Steelers won Super Bowl X the following year, he sacked Roger Staubach three times. Though his pass-rushing style was often described as "free-wheeling and reckless," he was remarkably consistent and undeniably effective.

Bob Carroll

JOE GREENE
Defensive Tackle (1969–81)

Pro Bowls (10), All-Pro (5),
Steelers MVP (1970),
NFL Defensive Player of the Year (1972, 1974),
NFL Defensive Rookie of the Year (1969),
Pro Football Hall of Fame (1987)

He had a devastating influence. He was just unrelenting. He refused to lose. And he made huge plays when they had to be made. He was just an awesome addition to our squad.

Andy Russell

on "Mean Joe" Greene

◇ ◇ ◇

He was the dominant factor. He was one of the rare guys who could change the complexion of the game all by himself. Football is the ultimate team sport, but he could make the difference in a ball game.

Mike Webster

on Greene

ERNIE STAUTNER
Defensive Tackle (1950–63)
Pro Bowls (9), All-Pro (4),
Pro Football Hall of Fame (1969)

He acted as if he was still trying to make good, 14 years after he broke into the league.

Bill McPeak
end (1949–57)/assistant coach (1956–58),
on Hall of Famer Ernie Stautner

The only jersey number that has been officially retired in the franchise's 73-year history is Ernie Stautner's number 70.

Norm Vargo

BILL McPEAK
Defensive End (1949–57)
Pro Bowls (3)

Bill McPeak was a pretty good end in his time and you might find a supportive argument from some of his peers about putting him on a Steelers all-time team over Dwight White.

Ed Bouchette

JACK HAM
Linebacker (1971–82)
Pro Bowls (8), All-Pro (6),
NFL Defensive Player of the Year
(1975, *Football News*),
Pro Football Hall of Fame (1988)

Jack Ham was a brilliant player. He didn't make mistakes, knew the game, and anticipated well. Plus, he was an explosive talent, probably the fastest Steeler in five yards—not in the forty, but he had an incredible explosion off the blocker. And he'd make it look easy. It was astounding how good he was. He was the best linebacker I ever saw— absolutely unbeatable.

Andy Russell

◇ ◇ ◇

As one observer put it, it was as if Jack Ham was on real time and everyone else was on seven-second delay.

Abby Mendelson

JACK LAMBERT

Middle Linebacker (1974–84)

Pro Bowls (9), All-Pro (8),
Steelers MVP (1976, 1981),
NFL Defensive Player of the Year (1976),
NFL Defensive Rookie of the Year (1974),
Pro Football Hall of Fame (1990)

When you start talking about attitude and focus, Jack Lambert is the epitome. He was the most focused individual I've ever had. He'd go on the practice field and there was no nonsense. It was get the job done. And he had the ability, at six-foot-four, to win the battle of hitting.

Chuck Noll

Jack Lambert, he'd pull his own teammates out of the way so he could get to the guy first.

Ted "The Mad Stork" Hendricks

Baltimore Colts/Oakland Raiders
Hall of Fame linebacker

ANDY RUSSELL

Linebacker (1963, 1966–76)

Pro Bowls (7), All-Pro (1975),
Steelers MVP (1971)

No professional athlete ever went through a wider swing of experiences. He was an All-Pro linebacker on some of the classic Pittsburgh disasters but also played in the first two Super Bowl triumphs. He never missed a game in 13 seasons.

Robert Oates Jr.

on Andy Russell

MEL BLOUNT

Cornerback (1970–83)

Pro Bowls (5), All-Pro (4),
NFL Defensive MVP (1975), Steelers MVP (1975),
Pro Football Hall of Fame (1989)

He's still the best ever to play the game. There's no one who comes close. With Mel Blount's speed, anticipation, height, and reach, nobody could get away from him.

Bud Carson

JACK BUTLER
Free Safety (1951–59)
Pro Bowls (4), All-Pro (3)

Some said only Hall of Fame defensive back Dick "Night Train" Lane was Butler's equal in the 1950s, and he finished his career in 1959 with 52 interceptions. Only Emlen Tunnell and Lane had more at the time. Tunnell called Butler "a defensive genius."

Jim J. Campbell
writer/historian

DONNIE SHELL
Strong Safety (1974–87)
Pro Bowls (5), All-Pro (3),
Steelers MVP (1980)

He put up numbers like no other strong safety and tackled with such ferocity, a writer punned, "He just leaves 'em Shell-shocked." Shell was so good for so long only ironman center Mike Webster played more games in a Steelers uniform than Shell's 201.

Jim J. Campbell

ROD WOODSON

Cornerback (1987–96)

Pro Bowls (7), All-Pro (4),
NFL 75th Anniversary All-Time Team (1994),
NFL Defensive Player of the Year (1993),
Steelers MVP (1988, 1990, 1993)

Rod Woodson is a tremendous athletic talent. He is a very good student of football and is a hard worker. Attitude, motivation, and determination—all those things come when Rod gets on the football field. He doesn't settle for anything less than perfection.

Carnell Lake

◇ ◇ ◇

His range is phenomenal. He's probably as good as there is in the National Football League.

Rich Gannon
former Oakland Raiders All-Pro quarterback

PAT BRADY
Punter (1952–54)

Pat Brady was the greatest kicker I've seen, and I've seen 'em all. People used to come out before the games just to watch him punt in practice.

Ernie Stautner

GARY ANDERSON
Kicker (1982–94)

Pro Bowls (3), All-Pro (1985),
Steelers MVP (1983),
NFL's all-time scoring leader

Gary's the most-respected kicker who's been through this league.

Jeff Reed
kicker (2002–)

LYNN CHANDNOIS

Kick Returner (1950–56)

Pro Bowls (2),
Washington Touchdown Club's
NFL Player of the Year (1952)

It's in the clutch that the long-legged, 205-pound Chandnois is most likely to come through. In the matter of kickoff returns, Chandnois has no peer.

Pat Livingston

Lynn had everything: size, speed, and shiftiness. If Chuck Noll had coached Chandnois, he'd be in the Hall of Fame.

Jerry Nuzum

halfback (1948–51)

CHUCK NOLL

Head Coach (1969–91)

Super Bowl championships (4),
Pro Football Hall of Fame (1993)

During Chuck Noll's 23-year career with the Steelers, the team won four Super Bowls and never went more than four years without making the playoffs.

Joe Horrigan

You can say anything you want about the great players we had, but if we didn't have Chuck Noll, we wouldn't have been successful. He was able to make players believe that we had a championship football team.

Jack Ham

9

THE GREAT STEELERS TEAMS

There were more great players on the 1974 club than the Steelers had in the previous 40 years combined.

Andrew O'Toole

Talent-laden Pittsburgh became an awe-some scoring machine in 1952. It tallied 300 points. That was the greatest total ever rolled up by a Pittsburgh team in its NFL history, for a twelve-game schedule.

Joe Tucker

*32-year Steelers
broadcaster/author*

Bobby Layne turned us into a football team. He's the only guy who could have made so much difference so fast.

Buddy Parker

*on the 1958 Steelers who went
7–4–1 behind future Hall of Fame
quarterback Bobby Layne,
acquired from Detroit after
helping guide the Lions to three
NFL titles*

I call them the Gashouse Gang. I hear their coach puts beer on their bus. But when you've played against them, your body is sore for days. They leave you black and blue.

Jim Brown
Cleveland Browns Hall of Fame fullback,
on the 1963 Steelers, who came within a win of claiming the Eastern Division title

What emerged was a team. Guys who believed that we could do things. Success breeds success.

Rocky Bleier
on the 1974 Steelers, after being ousted from the playoffs in 1972 by the perfect Miami Dolphins and by Oakland in 1973

The toughest part of winning Super Bowl IX was that we had to go out the next year and play every game like it was the Super Bowl. Every Sunday, every team was after us. But that's how we surpassed a lot of teams, how we were able to make it two years in a row.

L. C. Greenwood

It's a tribute to Mr. Rooney, Dan Rooney, Chuck Noll, and Joe Greene that even though we won Super Bowls, everybody didn't come unglued and think they were a star and start bickering for the money, prestige, and recognition.

George Perles
*on the seventies' Super Bowl
champion teams*

We could play the game anyway you wanted to play it. If we played the Oakland Raiders, who were a physical team, and you had to go toe-to-toe—we could do that. The Dallas Cowboys, who we played twice in four years in the Super Bowl, were more of a finesse team, with formation changing, all kinds of different looks for your defense; we had the ability to do that as well. I think that may have set us apart from other teams.

Jack Ham

on the dynasty teams of the '70s

You make mistakes and it can crush you mentally. But this team does not crush.

Chuck Noll

on his 1975 Steelers

No one could move the sticks. We won ten in a row. Five shutouts—and shutouts in the NFL are unheard of. No field goals?

Andy Russell

on the 1976 Steelers, thought by many to be the best of the dynasty teams. Though they lost the AFC Championship Game to Oakland, in their nine consecutive wins to close the regular season, Pittsburgh gave up just 28 points

◇　◇　◇

Offensive coordinators worried not just about trying to game-plan them, but about how not to lose a player. You worried about losing a quarterback or a running back. Those guys played you life and death. The Steelers would demoralize you.

Stan Walters

twelve-year offensive tackle with Cincinnati, Philadelphia (1972–83), on the Steel Curtain defense of the 1970s

We would ultimately wear teams down. It was very difficult for teams to throw on us, because you had to beat Mel Blount, J. T. Thomas, Ron Johnson, or one of those safeties. Underneath we had the best and fastest linebackers. You had better get the ball off in a hurry or you were going to get hit by me, L. C. Greenwood, Dwight White, or Ernie Holmes. This went on and on and on. You had to deal with us over and over and over and over and over.

Joe Greene

on the '70s dynasty teams

In the '70s, the Pittsburgh Steelers played the best defense that has ever been played.

Dan Rooney

When pressed, Chuck Noll allowed that the 1979 Steelers team was the best to date.

Bill Chastain

sportswriter/author

The Pittsburgh team from the seventies is probably the best of all time. I put them up against any team. As good as Bill Walsh and Joe Montana were (the 49ers of the eighties), Pittsburgh would win. . . . Defensively they had no weaknesses. They could cover. And they had so many Hall of Fame guys, like the old Green Bay Packers. The Vince Lombardi era would be the only team to probably give them a run.

Vince Ferragamo

former Los Angeles Rams quarterback who lost to the '79 Steelers in Super Bowl XIV

They're the best team in football. What they did, we didn't do. They outplayed us. They're the team of the '70s.

Larry Little

*Miami Dolphins Hall of Fame guard/tackle,
following the 34–14 AFC divisional playoff victory over Miami in 1979*

◇ ◇ ◇

This year we realized that when we put it all together, there wasn't a team in the National Football League that could beat us.

Yancy Thigpen

on the 1995 Super Bowl XXX-bound Steelers

◇ ◇ ◇

I'm impressed with their superb athleticism and their great talent. They're stronger, bigger, and faster than we were. They would beat us.

Andy Russell

comparing the defenses of his dynasty teams of the 1970s with the 1995 AFC champions

You watch Hines Ward play. You watch Jerome Bettis play. You watch the players Bill Cowher has surrounded himself with taking hits or giving hits and mixing it up, and they have big smiles from ear to ear. That's the mentality of this team.

Sean Morey
*flanker/special teams (2004–),
on the 2005 world champion
Steelers*

When it's do or die for us, this team gets down to the nitty gritty.

Ben Roethlisberger
on the 2005 Steelers

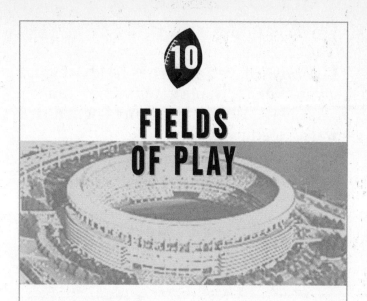

10

FIELDS OF PLAY

The plot of ground on which Three Rivers Stadium once stood was the former domain of the Pittsburgh Steelers. An arena of concrete that housed a team of steel, and the words scratched into its tempered metal read, "Abandon All Hope, Ye Who Enter Here."

Tom Danyluk

His boys played at Forbes Field, which, given Pennsylvania's autumnal rains, was generally a quagmire—when it wasn't iced over.

Abby Mendelson

on the venerable home of the Pittsburgh Pirates, shared by both the baseball Bucs and Art Rooney's football team of the same name, the forerunner of the Steelers from 1933 through '39

The Pirates franchise played its games in Forbes Field before crowds that rarely exceeded 20,000 viewers.

John Hogrogian

writer/researcher/Professional Football Researchers Association member

FAST FACT: The Pirates-Steelers played their home games at Forbes Field from 1933 through 1957 and at both Forbes Field and Pitt Stadium from 1958 through 1963.

The place was ours. We sat anywhere we wanted.

Joe Chiodo

*longtime fan,
who rode the streetcar to
sparsely attended early Pirates-
Steelers games at Forbes Field,
beginning in 1934–35*

◇ ◇ ◇

The Forbes Field baseball management bestowed shoddy treatment on the Steelers. The football club continually played second fiddle to Forbes Field's primary tenants, often time the Pirates wouldn't even allow the Steelers to practice on the playing field.

Andrew O'Toole

◇ ◇ ◇

I remember The Chief calling me in 1968 and telling me to come over for a photo op. He and I put a shovel around in some ugly field on the North Side, which is now Three Rivers Stadium.

Andy Russell

This is the place that enabled Pittsburgh to be called the City of Champions in the 1970s. This is the place that Joe Greene and Roberto Clemente graced.

Bob Smizik

sportswriter,
on Three Rivers Stadium

I watched Three Rivers Stadium implode on TV that day (February 11, 2001). They showed it over and over. The first seven or eight times, it didn't really faze me. Then after the ninth time, something hit me . . . I began to think of all the players and the coaches and the workouts and the great games. I spent so much time down there, trying to build something good, and then it was gone. I needed a moment, I really did.

Art Rooney Jr.

This is about an old friend, almost 29 and not long for the world. This is about a place no one is mourning when, in this case, there is good reason to do so. This is about Three Rivers Stadium, which won't make it to 31.

Bob Smizik

on Three Rivers Stadium

This is a stadium to mourn, a stadium that brought us a lifetime of thrills and memories. It's an oft-ridiculed ballpark that we never took to our hearts, but should have. It was too hard to get to and harder still to leave. And it housed baseball and football and so wasn't really right for either. But, oh, the memories, oh, the thrills.

Bob Smizik

Franco Harris took a bow at the ground-breaking ceremonies [for Heinz Field]. Nothing more need be said to bring to mind the most famous play in NFL history—The Immaculate Reception. It will be talked about as long as they play the game and it happened at Three Rivers.

Bob Smizik

The Steeler Nation was born here. So was Franco's Italian Army and the Terrible Towel. Yet no one is saying a word about its demise. No one is demanding a stay of execution. Nor should anyone. Time marches on. It's time for new stadiums, one for football, one for baseball.

Bob Smizik
on Three Rivers

The fans did themselves proud, letting the house that had treated them to so many thrills go with dignity. That surprised those who stereotype all Steeler fans as beery louts who use the North Shore as an outdoor urinal.

Robert Dvorchak

sportswriter,
on the ceremonial events during
and after the Steelers' final home
game at Three Rivers Stadium,
December 16, 2000

The mood was uniquely Pittsburgh. Where else could Hank Williams Jr. sing the National Anthem and a country tune, then be followed by the polka fight song they used to play in the '70s?

Robert Dvorchak

Coincidentally, the playground where Dan Rooney and his brothers once played football was a parking lot at Three Rivers Stadium.

Joe Horrigan

2000

Searchlights were shining on the new stadium rising just 65 feet away from the outer edge of Three Rivers. While some question the wisdom of leaving a stadium on which $26 million is still owed, it is the fans who paid the charter seat licenses to help pay for the new construction [of Heinz Field].

Robert Dvorchak

11

RIVALRIES

I kept my mouth shut and my helmet on when I went to Pittsburgh.

Joe "Turkey" Jones
*Cleveland Browns defensive end
(1970–71, 1973, 1975–78)*

Starting in 1950, the Cleveland Browns became a natural rival, located some 120 miles from Pittsburgh. Art Modell recognized the importance of the rivalry with Pittsburgh and twice insisted the Steelers and Browns be in the same division, during NFL realignment for 1967 and 1970.

Morris Eckhouse
author

For the people of Cleveland, when you beat Pittsburgh, it was almost like, "Screw the rest of the season." You can make or break your season just by beating them.

Doug Dieken
*Cleveland Browns tackle
(1971–84)*

You could really feel the crowd, and most players fed off that. Against Pittsburgh, there was a constant roar, even in between plays. That fills your body so full of adrenaline, and it gives you that extra effort. When that roar happens and you're running on a play, if you couldn't get to the ball carrier, you'd peel back and just drill somebody, even a lineman.

Jerry Sherk
former Cleveland Browns nose guard

The townspeople identified with it more than any other game, so when we played Pittsburgh, it was an unbelievable week. You could sense the mood of Cleveland before and after the game. If we won the game, the town would be on fire and people would go to work for a couple weeks in a positive mood. And if we lost the game, it would be the exact opposite.

Jerry Sherk

on the Pittsburgh rivalry

It was like a playoff game. You don't want to think you cranked it up to a higher level, but you did. There was a lot of pride and honor on the line. And it was always physical. We got Jack Lambert thrown out of two or three games, which was probably the best part of our game plan.

Doug Dieken
on the Pittsburgh Steelers rivalry

The doorway to the championship out of the AFC always went through Oakland.

Joe Greene

The Immaculate Reception was what set the stage. A controversial call. All the makings of a rivalry right there. That game was already locked up.

Ted Hendricks

In the 1970s, the mention of Pittsburgh and Oakland meant one thing—playoff football. In an amazing five-year span from 1972–76, the teams met annually in either an AFC divisional or championship game. The final three were for the conference championship, with the first two being taken by the Steelers and the last by the Raiders. All three times, the winner went on to capture the Super Bowl.

NFL.com

September 10, 2002

The Raiders could beat you any kind of way—offense, defense, special teams. To me they were the big bad bully.

Joe Greene

Art Shell on that left side was tough, and so was Dave Casper. Casper was just a physical tight end. You'd bang him around and he'd bounce right back up. No one ever shows that they took a good shot, it's a macho thing. Phil Villapiano on their defense, he was another tough guy.

Jack Ham

For me, as a participant and as a fan, that was the beauty of the game, in that we could play the Raiders and be on top of our game and they would be on top of their game, and the result would be that whoever watched it would be watching a pretty good football game.

Joe Greene

When we played the Eagles, it would usually get a little rough and dirty. Pittsburgh and Philadelphia were in the same state, so it became a real intense rivalry. They always used to accuse each other of hurting a ball player in the game before, and there would be talk about how next time it's your turn. That's how it went, back and forth.

Dale Dodrill
*nose guard/middle linebacker
(1951–59)*

In 1954, the Eagles had to be advised to wear their helmets on their way onto the field because bottles would be thrown at their heads.

Roy Blount Jr.
writer/author

Bengals-Steelers last year replaced Baltimore Ravens-Steelers as the most anticipated game in the division, and what happened in 2005 should heat it up more. Cincinnati dethroned the Steelers by winning their first division title since 1990, virtually locking it up with an upset victory in Heinz Field.

Ed Bouchette

FAST FACT: The Bengals iced the AFC North crown with their 38–31 victory over Pittsburgh on December 4.

The Steelers beat the Bengals in Cincinnati in the first round of the 2005 playoffs, as Kimo von Oelhoffen knocked Bengals quarterback Carson Palmer out with a low hit that tore his ACL.

Ed Bouchette

The Bengals-Steelers rivalry has reached a point not seen since Chuck Noll refused to shake Sam Wyche's hand after games.

Ed Bouchette

That's a big game. Why would I want our game in Pittsburgh to be on a Thursday night to open the 2006 season? We'll play there when we play there. . . . That stadium is going to be . . . well, depending on what time it starts, whether or not they'll still be sober. But it's going to be loud, it'll be a loud place.

Marvin Lewis

Cincinnati Bengals head coach

FANS

Steelers fans are unlike any other football following. Those teams of the '70s—they could have played a game in Zanzibar, and there'd be two hundred fans waiting for them at the hotel when they arrived. It's practically unheard of in my experience to find a fellow who's left the city, or been transferred, to adopt another city's football team. They're Steelers fans for life.

Myron Cope

They're awesome. You can't ask for better fans than we have. Football season, people are just rockin' it like crazy. It's perfect.

Kordell Stewart

Three Rivers Stadium is a hard place for other people to win. Our people are a tremendous advantage here. Our people are very loud, very supportive. I wouldn't want to be on the other side.

Bill Cowher

The true fans like defense, the hard-hitting, the blue-collar mentality. And we are an attack defense—Pittsburgh and our defense is like a hand in a glove.

Rod Woodson

The fans are a special part of Steeler history. They're passionate. They want to win, and they want to go to the Super Bowl every year. But they never give up on the team. I think their loyalty and consistency is remarkable.

Tom Donahoe

former director of football operations

◇ ◇ ◇

We won it for the fans.

Mike Webster

◇ ◇ ◇

They could boo us and talk about us, but they wouldn't let anybody else do it. There were times when they would make that stadium rock: DEE-fense! DEE-fense! DEE-fense!

Joe Greene

The spirit of the town was incredible. Franco's Italian Army was a big part of that. Bringing in the fans, and getting them behind us—I really enjoyed it.

Franco Harris

◇ ◇ ◇

Myron Cope elevated what for many was a used yellow dishrag into an objet d'art.

Abby Mendelson

*on Cope's enduring fan creation,
the Terrible Towel, that debuted
in November 1975*

◇ ◇ ◇

They gave us that extra spark. I loved to respond when they were calling my name. I always wanted to do something positive.

Louis Lipps

*wide receiver (1984–91),
on the Steelers throng roaring
"L-o-o-o-o-o-o-u-u-u-u" during
home games*

Steelers football, to a great many Steelers fans, is a religious experience. You put them in the privacy of their homes, or in a seat two hundred feet away, and the metamorphosis is startling.

Mark Malone

quarterback (1980–87)

The thing that makes Three Rivers Stadium great is the Hall of Fame fans.

Chuck Noll

We're coming from everywhere. We play with 15 guys in the huddle. We have guys parachuting from airplanes, fans coming from out of the stands to help us go after people.

Kevin Greene

We're an extension of this city and of the fan who watches us play.

Bill Cowher

They don't throw anything at you; they just talk a lot of trash. They're all looking at you like, "You all know you're going to get beat, right?"

Reinard Wilson
former Cincinnati Bengals
defensive end/linebacker,
on Steelers fans

Don't ever place your hand on a Pittsburgh Steeler fan.

Song lyric
from a Charlie Daniels tune

Steelers fans travel well. They always have. . . . They traversed the 285 miles from Pittsburgh to southeastern Michigan [for Super Bowl XL] by car, hung out, partied, and twirled their Terrible Towels, many without even attempting to buy a ticket to the game.

Larry Weisman
USA TODAY

I was trying to think of something different to wear. The seamstress just used a pajama pattern to make them.

Roy R. Doty
Steelers fan,
who wore a body suit comprised
of fifteen Terrible Towels to
Super Bowl XL

Everywhere the Steelers went, they saw their colors carried or worn by vociferous fans of the Black and Gold. Their numbers dwarfed those of the Seattle fans. It would not have been surprising to find out that Super Bowl XL was being contested by two teams called the Steelers, so numerous were their supporters.

Larry Weisman

THE LOCKER ROOM

It is an end. It's been an incredible ride. I came back to win a championship, and now I have to bid farewell. It's totally, totally a blessing. I'm probably the luckiest football player who ever played.

Jerome Bettis

on his 13-year NFL career that culminated in victory in his final game, Super Bowl XL

It was in Pittsburgh that Art Rooney bought his $2,500 National Football League franchise in 1933, during the Depression, when people didn't have enough money for footwear, much less football.

Abby Mendelson

In the early years, The Chief operated the Steelers out of a hotel office and a pocket notebook. He brought his five sons into the family sports businesses and was succeeded at the Steelers by Dan, his eldest.

Abby Mendelson
on Art Rooney

In January of 1939, Byron White went to England to begin his Rhodes Scholarship at Oxford university. His stay was cut short. When Great Britain declared war against Germany in September, American students were sent home. White had an enviable fallback plan. He entered Yale Law School and played pro football on weekends in 1940 and 1941 with the Detroit Lions, which had purchased negotiating rights from the Pirates, which became the Steelers in 1940.

John Hogrogian

Sometimes with the lessons of life, you have to get knocked down before you get back up. He's just very fortunate. This was one of those lessons that could have been devastating.

Bill Cowher

following Ben Roethlisberger's controversial motorcycle crash in June 2006

◇ ◇ ◇

I have gained a new perspective on life. . . . If I ever ride again, it certainly will be with a helmet.

Ben Roethlisberger

upon his release from the hospital

◇ ◇ ◇

Geezus, if he's going to wear a helmet when he plays football, you'd think he'd wear a helmet when he's tooling around town on a mini-rocket launcher. What's everybody worried about, helmet hair?

Gene Wojciechowski

ESPN.com, on Roethlisberger's bike accident

He was a brilliant and eccentric free spirit, a better raconteur than football coach.

John Hogrogian

on early Steelers player-head coach Johnny Blood, "The Vagabond Halfback," and a Hall of Famer

Buddy Parker never taught me anything. I was scared and nervous and all screwed up. He never even told me I was lousy. At least, if he had, he would have shown me he knew I was alive.

Len Dawson

quarterback (1957–59)/ Hall of Fame QB with Kansas City Chiefs (1962–75), on his three-year frustration in Pittsburgh, during which he threw a total of just 17 passes, playing mostly behind veteran Bobby Layne

My attitude was to bring in so many good players that the coaches couldn't screw the team up. That might've been an immature approach, but that's exactly how I felt. We were trying to build a team, but we wanted it to be a lasting team.

Art Rooney Jr.

I've campaigned for years to get him elected to the Pro Football Hall of Fame. I don't vote for owners and administrators very often. They should have their own wing, separate from the players. But Art Jr. would get my vote in a heartbeat. Look at all the talent he assembled. His '74 draft is the greatest in NFL history.

Paul Zimmerman
writer/author and Hall of Fame selector,
on Art Rooney Jr.

The Steelers had always been run as a Jenga-type operation in the way it collected and secured its young talent—bring in the players, erect the foundation, while at the same time pulling out potentially key parts and throwing away gobs of valuable draft choices. Coaches came and went, but inevitably by each season's end the inspectors would come and hammer up the condemned signs on a teetering structure.

Tom Danyluk

*on the pre-Chuck Noll days
in Steelertown*

Rooney's trademark cigar and smile never left him. When he felt his team's losses, he suffered like a Pittsburgher—in silence.

Abby Mendelson

In 1970 we were offered a bundle for the pick we used on Terry Bradshaw, but we turned it down. When you have the chance to pick a great football player like Bradshaw, you pick him. In the old days we might have made that deal.

Art Rooney Jr.

Everybody beats on him. [Giants linebacker] Sam Huff treats him like a dog.

Buddy Dial
end (1959–63),
on fullback John Henry Johnson

Sometimes if you make kicks early in the game, you don't have to make them late.

Gary Anderson

He gets us fired up. He's our emotional leader. He talks but he backs it up with his play.

Casey Hampton

on Joey Porter

◇ ◇ ◇

Marion Motley came to Pittsburgh at the end of his career, and I can still remember the first time I saw him practice. It hurt to see him run with the knees he had.

Dale Dodrill

on the great Hall of Fame fullback who played most of his pro years with Cleveland

◇ ◇ ◇

I called my own plays. Now they have microphones in the helmet. They (QBs) don't call the plays. Don't even think anymore. "Call timeout. Got a bad microphone." I say, get rid of that stuff.

Terry Bradshaw

You could almost see the transformation. He made the players believe in themselves again—that they could be winners.

Steelers club official
after Bobby Layne's arrival in Pittsburgh, in 1958

In a 1961 game, John Henry Johnson applied his forearm to the physiognomy of Rams captain Les Richter, breaking Richter's jaw. Later in the game, Johnson was laid out on the L.A. sideline when a procession of Rams came after him. Johnson grabbed a sideline marker and began bashing it against the helmets of his antagonists and survived unscathed.

Austin Murphy

I went to my twentieth high school class reunion. That was kind of special, after twenty years, to come back and be the head coach of the professional football team in the same city that you grew up in. That was pretty unique.

Bill Cowher

I am one of those people who can say, not that I was the very best, but that *we* were. We did something together that no one can take away from us, and that we can't personally say, "It's mine."

Terry Bradshaw

Who could have ever imagined a turf toe would bring down the meanest Steeler of all? I couldn't. After all these years, I still can't believe it.

Jack Ham

on the career-ending injury to Hall of Fame middle linebacker Jack Lambert in 1984

In truth, I never felt I was the leader of the offense. Mike Webster was. He led by example. He would turn around, at times, and suggest audibles I ought to call. He knew everybody's blocking assignment. He was the quarterback of the offensive line and called out all adjustments. He helped me through a few games, I'll admit that.

Terry Bradshaw

We just had too many good football players. You can't beat talent.

Joe Greene

It was literally a vacation with pay, the most fun I ever had playing football. You'd stick your head in the huddle and the smell of alcohol would hang there till hell froze over. But you'd just raise up and go "ahhh," and get a breath of fresh air.

Bill Dudley

*on his rookie season (1942)
with the Steelers, in which he led
the NFL in rushing, punt return
yards, and kickoff return average*

You try to control your mind, but no matter what you do, you never are able to escape Sunday morning. At least during the week, you can drink. Come Saturday night and Sunday morning, you can't even do that.

Bruce Van Dyke
guard (1967–73)/
1974 Pro Bowler,
on dealing with pregame tension

There isn't a moment from the time I go into that dressing room until the game is over, that I'm not praying. People think I'm talking to myself, but I'm praying.

Ernie Holmes
defensive tackle (1972–77)

Just get me to Detroit.

Jerome Bettis

to teammates before the start of the 2005 AFC Championship Game at Denver. The Steelers didn't disappoint, burying Jake Plummer and the Broncos 34–17 to reach their second Super Bowl since the seventies' dynasty years

He called me and said, "Listen. Enjoy it and have fun because you never know if you're going to come back.

Ben Roethlisberger

on a conversation with Dan Marino the week of Super Bowl XL. Marino, an NFL prodigy in his second NFL season, 1984, took his Miami Dolphins to Super Bowl XIX that year, losing to the San Francisco 49ers. He never got back to another title game

Hair We Go!

Banner at Super Bowl XL

in tribute to long-locked Pro Bowl safety Troy Polamalu

It's official, like the referee's whistle.

Jerome Bettis

on his farewell to pro football following the Steelers' 21–10 win over Seattle in Super Bowl XL. Bettis exited the game as the NFL's No. 5 all-time rusher

STEELERS
WORLD CHAMPION
ROSTERS

*A*t one point, in the sixties, head coach Buddy Parker forecast that whenever Steelers fortunes changed, it would be for a run of ten years. His prognostication eventually culminated in the NFL dynasty team of the seventies that pounded out a still-amazing four Super Bowl titles in six years.

It would be sixteen years before Pittsburgh got back to the big stage, and another ten after that before they gained a fifth Super Bowl crown, the instant-legend One for the Thumb that capped 2005.

Many have contributed to the Steelers' championship ways. It wasn't about stars, though there were plenty, but about team, the crux of the Noll- and Cowher-based philosophies.

The world champion Black and Gold:

1974

13–3–1

(includes 32–14 AFC playoff win over Buffalo,
24–13 AFC Championship Game win over Oakland,
and 16–6 Super Bowl IX victory over Minnesota)

Chuck Noll, *head coach*

Allen, Jimmy	DB		**Harris, Franco**	**RB**
Bleier, Rocky	**RB**		Harrison, Reggie	RB
Blount, Mel	**CB**		**Holmes, Ernie**	**DT**
Bradley, Ed	LB		Kellum, Marv	LB
Bradshaw, Terry	**QB**		**Kolb, Jon**	**T**
Brown, Larry	**TE**		**Lambert, Jack**	**MLB**
Clack, Jim	**G**		**Lewis, Frank**	**WR**
Conn, Dick	DB		**Mansfield, Ray**	**C**
Davis, Charles	DT		McMakin, John	TE
Davis, Samuel	G		**Mullins, Gerry**	**G**
Davis, Steve	RB		Pearson, Preston	B
Druschel, Rich	G-T		Reavis, Dave	DT
Edwards, Glen	**FS**		**Russell, Andy**	**OLB**
Furness, Steve	DT		**Shanklin, Ronnie**	**WR**
Garrett, Reggie	WR		Shell, Donnie	SS
Gerela, Roy	K		Stallworth, John	WR
Gilliam, Joe	QB		Swann, Lynn	WR
Gravelle, Gordon	**T**		**Thomas, J. T.**	**CB**
Greene, Joe	**DT**		Toews, Loren	LB
Greenwood, L. C.	**DE**		**Wagner, Mike**	**SS**
Grossman, Randy	TE		Walden, Bobby	P
Ham, Jack	**OLB**		Webster, Mike	C
Hanratty, Terry	QB		**White, Dwight**	**DE**
			Wolf, James	DE

Starters in bold

1975

15–2

(includes 28–10 AFC playoff win over Baltimore, 16–10 AFC Championship Game win over Oakland, and 21–17 Super Bowl X victory over Dallas)

Chuck Noll, *head coach*

Allen, Jimmy	DB	Hanratty, Terry	QB
Banaszak, John	DE/DT	**Harris, Franco**	**RB**
Bleier, Rocky	**RB**	Harrison, Reggie	RB
Blount, Mel	**CB**	**Holmes, Ernie**	**DT**
Bradley, Ed	LB	Kellum, Marv	LB
Bradshaw, Terry	**QB**	**Kolb, Jon**	**T**
Brown, Dave	DB	**Lambert, Jack**	**MLB**
Brown, Larry	**TE**	Lewis, Frank	WR
Clack, Jim	**G**	**Mansfield, Ray**	**C**
Collier, Mike	RB	**Mullins, Gerry**	**G**
Davis, Samuel	G	Reavis, Dave	DT
Edwards, Glen	**FS**	**Russell, Andy**	**OLB**
Fuqua, John	RB	Shell, Donnie	SS
Furness, Steve	DT	**Stallworth, John**	**WR**
Garrett, Reggie	WR	**Swann, Lynn**	**WR**
Gerela, Roy	K	**Thomas, J. T.**	**CB**
Gilliam, Joe	QB	Toews, Loren	LB
Gravelle, Gordon	**T**	**Wagner, Mike**	**SS**
Greene, Joe	**DT**	Walden, Bobby	P
Greenwood, L. C.	**DE**	Webster, Mike	C
Grossman, Randy	TE	**White, Dwight**	**DE**
Ham, Jack	**OLB**		

1978

17–2

(includes 33–10 AFC playoff win over Denver,
34–5 AFC Championship Game win over Houston,
and 35–31 Super Bowl XIII victory over Dallas)

Chuck Noll, *head coach*

Anderson, Fred	DE		**Harris, Franco**	**RB**
Anderson, Larry	DB		**Johnson, Ronald**	**CB**
Banaszak, John	**DE**		**Kolb, Jon**	**T**
Beasley, Tom	DE/DT		Kruczek, Mike	QB
Bell, Theo	WR		**Lambert, Jack**	**MLB**
Bleier, Rocky	**RB**		Mandich, Jim	TE
Blount, Mel	**CB**		Moser, Rick	RB
Bradshaw, Terry	**QB**		**Mullins, Gerry**	**G**
Brown, Larry	TE/OT		Oldham, Ray	DB
Cole, Robin	LB		Petersen, Ted	T/C
Colquitt, Craig	P		**Pinney, Ray**	**T**
Courson, Steve	G		**Shell, Donnie**	**SS**
Cunningham, Bennie	TE		Smith, Jim	WR
Davis, Samuel	**G**		**Stallworth, John**	**WR**
Deloplaine, Jack	RB		Stoudt, Cliff	QB
Dungy, Tony	DB		**Swann, Lynn**	**WR**
Dunn, Gary	DT/NT		Thornton, Sidney	RB
Furness, Steve	**DT**		**Toews, Loren**	**OLB**
Gerela, Roy	K		**Wagner, Mike**	**FS**
Greene, Joe	**DT**		**Webster, Mike**	**C**
Greenwood, L. C.	**DE**		White, Dwight	DE
Grossman, Randy	**TE**		Winston, Dennis	LB
Ham, Jack	**OLB**			

1979

15–4

(includes 34–14 AFC playoff win over Miami, 27–13 AFC Championship Game win over Houston, and 31–19 Super Bowl XIV victory over Los Angeles)

Chuck Noll, *head coach*

Anderson, Anthony	RB	**Harris, Franco**	**RB**
Anderson, Larry	DB	Hawthorne, Greg	RB
Bahr, Matt	K	**Johnson, Ronald**	**CB**
Banaszak, John	**DE**	**Kolb, Jon**	**T**
Beasley, Tom	DE/DT	Kruczek, Mike	QB
Bell, Theo	WR	**Lambert, Jack**	**MLB**
Bleier, Rocky	**RB**	Moser, Rick	RB
Blount, Mel	**CB**	**Mullins, Gerry**	**G**
Bradshaw, Terry	**QB**	Petersen, Ted	T/C
Brown, Larry	**T**	**Shell, Donnie**	**SS**
Cole, Robin	**OLB**	Smith, Jim	WR
Colquitt, Craig	P	**Stallworth, John**	**WR**
Courson, Steve	G	Stoudt, Cliff	QB
Cunningham, Bennie	**TE**	**Swann, Lynn**	**WR**
Davis, Samuel	**G**	**Thomas, J. T.**	**FS**
Dornbrook, Thom	G/C	Thornton, Sidney	RB
Dunn, Gary	**DT**	Toews, Loren	LB
Furness, Steve	DT	Valentine, Zack	LB
Graves, Tom	LB	**Webster, Mike**	**C**
Greene, Joe	**DT**	White, Dwight	DE
Greenwood, L. C.	**DE**	**Winston, Dennis**	**OLB**
Grossman, Randy	TE	Woodruff, Dwayne	CB
Ham, Jack	OLB		

2005

15–5

(includes 31–17 AFC Wild Card win over Cincinnati, 21–18 AFC Divisional Playoff win over Indianapolis, 34–17 AFC Championship Game win over Denver, and 21–10 Super Bowl XL victory over Seattle)

Bill Cowher, *head coach*

	Pos.	Ht.	Wt.	College
Batch, Charlie	QB	6–2	216	Eastern Michigan
Bettis, Jerome	RB	5–11	255	Notre Dame
Brooks, Barrett	OT	6–4	325	Kansas State
Carter, Tyrone	S	5–8	190	Minnesota
Colclough, Ricardo	CB	5–11	186	Tusculum
Essex, Trai	OT	6–4	324	Northwestern
Faneca, Alan	**OG**	**6–5**	**307**	**LSU**
Farrior, James	**LB**	**6–2**	**243**	**Virginia**
Foote, Larry	**LB**	**6–0**	**239**	**Michigan**
Gardocki, Chris	P	6–1	192	Clemson
Haggans, Clark	**LB**	**6–4**	**243**	**Colorado State**
Hampton, Casey	**DT**	**6–1**	**325**	**Texas**
Harrison, Arnold	LB	6–3	236	Georgia
Harrison, James	LB	6–0	242	Kent State
Hartings, Jeff	**C**	**6–3**	**299**	**Penn State**
Haynes, Verron	RB	5–9	222	Georgia
Hoke, Chris	DT	6–3	296	BYU
Hope, Chris	**S**	**5–11**	**206**	**Florida State**
Iwuoma, Chidi	CB	5–8	184	California
Keisel, Brett	DE	6–5	285	BYU
Kemoeatu, Chris	OG	6–3	344	Utah
Kirschke, Travis	DE	6–3	298	UCLA
Kreider, Dan	**FB**	**5–11**	**255**	**New Hampshire**

Kriewaldt, Clint	LB	6–1	248	Wis.-Stevens Pt.
Logan, Mike	S	6–1	211	West Virginia
Maddox, Tommy	QB	6–4	219	UCLA
Mays, Lee	WR	6–2	193	Texas-El Paso
McFadden, Bryant	CB	5–11	190	Florida State
Miller, Heath	**TE**	**6–5**	**256**	**Virginia**
Morey, Sean	WR	5–11	200	Brown
Nua, Shaun	DE	6–5	280	BYU
Okobi, Chukky	C	6–1	318	Purdue
Parker, Willie	**RB**	**5–10**	**209**	**North Carolina**
Polamalu, Troy	**S**	**5–10**	**212**	**Southern Cal**
Porter, Joey	**LB**	**6–3**	**250**	**Colorado State**
Randle El, Antwaan	**WR**	**5–10**	**192**	**Indiana**
Reed, Jeff	K	5–11	232	North Carolina
Roethlisberger, Ben	**QB**	**6–5**	**241**	**Miami (Ohio)**
Simmons, Kendall	**OG**	**6–3**	**319**	**Auburn**
Smith, Aaron	**DE**	**6–5**	**298**	**Northern Colorado**
Smith, Marvel	**OT**	**6–5**	**321**	**Arizona State**
Staley, Duce	RB	5–11	242	South Carolina
Starks, Max	**OT**	**6–8**	**337**	**Florida**
Taylor, Ike	**CB**	**6–1**	**191**	**La.-Lafayette**
Townsend, Deshea	**CB**	**5–10**	**190**	**Alabama**
Tuman, Jerame	TE	6–4	253	Michigan
von Oelhoffen, Kimo	**DE**	**6–4**	**299**	**Boise State**
Wallace, Rian	LB	6–2	243	Temple
Ward, Hines	**WR**	**6–0**	**205**	**Georgia**
Warren, Greg	LS	6–3	252	North Carolina
Washington, Nate	WR	6–1	185	Tiffin
Williams, Willie	CB	5–9	194	Western Carolina
Wilson, Cedrick	WR	5–10	183	Tennessee

Reserve/Injured:

Frazier, Andre	LB	6–5	234	Cincinnati
Morgan, Quincy	WR	6–1	215	Kansas State
Stuvaints, Russell	S	6–0	210	Youngstown State

BIBLIOGRAPHY

Anderson, Dave. "Johnny Unitas." *Great Pro Quarterbacks*. New York: Grosset & Dunlap, 1972.

Bell, Jarrett and Nate Davis, et al. "Motown looks like Steel City." *USA TODAY*. 6 Feb. 2006: 6C.

Bergeron, Elena. "2005 Report Card: Ben Roethlisberger." *ESPN The Magazine*. 13 Feb. 2006: 96.

Blount, Roy Jr. *About Three Bricks Shy of a Load: A Highly Irregular Lowdown on the Year the Pittsburgh Steelers Were Super but Missed the Bowl*. Boston, Mass.: Little, Brown and Company, 1974.

Bouchette, Ed. *The Pittsburgh Steelers*. New York: St. Martin's Press, 1994.

Bouchette, Ed. "Steelers Rally Past Bears, 37-34 (*Pittsburgh Post-Gazette* reprint)." Fitzgerald, Francis J., ed. *Greatest Moments in Pittsburgh Steelers History*. Louisville, Ky.: AdCraft Sports Marketing, 1996.

Bouchette, Ed. "Bounce in the End Zone Goes the Steelers' Way (*Pittsburgh Post-Gazette* reprint)." Fitzgerald, Francis J., ed. *Greatest Moments in Pittsburgh Steelers History*. Louisville, Ky.: AdCraft Sports Marketing, 1996.

Bradshaw, Terry with David Diles. *Terry Bradshaw: Man of Steel*. Grand Rapids, Mich.: Zondervan Publishing House, 1980.

Brady, Erik. "Cowher keeps jaw up for prize: Steeler coach needs Super Bowl trophy to complete his portrait." *USA Today*. 2 Feb. 2006: 2C.

Burchard, S.H. *Sports Star: Franco Harris*. New York: Harcourt Brace Jovanovich, Inc., 1976.

Campbell, Jim. "Oh, Those X's and O's! or the evolution of pro football strategy." *The Coffin Corner*, Vol. XIX, No. 4 (1997): 5, 7, 9, 11.

Carroll, Bob and Michael Gershman, et al. *Total Football II: The Official Encyclopedia of the National Football League*. New York: HarperCollins Publishers, 1999.

Carroll, Bob. "The Hall of Very Good 2004." *The Coffin Corner*, Vol. 26, No. 2, 2004: 16.

Chass, Murray. *Pittsburgh's Steelers: The Long Climb*. Englewood Cliffs, N.J.: Prentice-Hall, Inc., 1973.

Chastain, Bill. *Steel Dynasty: The Team that Changed the NFL*. Chicago, Ill.: Triumph Books, 2005.

Clary, Jack. *The Coffin Corner*. Volume XVI, 1994.

Clayton, John. "Steelers Register 3rd Super Bowl Victory (*Pittsburgh Press* reprint)." Fitzgerald, Francis J., ed. *Greatest Moments in Pittsburgh Steelers History*. Louisville, Ky.: AdCraft Sports Marketing, 1996.

Clayton, John. "Stallworth Makes the Call (*Pittsburgh Press* reprint)." Fitzgerald, Francis J., ed. *Greatest Moments in Pittsburgh Steelers History*. Louisville, Ky.: AdCraft Sports Marketing, 1996.

Collins, Bob. "Hard to Name an Equal for Layne." (*Indianapolis Star* reprint, 1982,) Roberts, Randy and David Welky, eds. *The Steelers Reader*. Pittsburgh, Pa.: University of Pittsburgh Press, 2001.

Cook, Ron. "Steelers Crush Jets, Clinch Wild-Card Spot (*Pittsburgh Press* reprint)." Fitzgerald, Francis J., ed. *Greatest Moments in Pittsburgh Steelers History*. Louisville, Ky.: AdCraft Sports Marketing, 1996.

Cook, Ron. "Steeler Triumph over Niners Is a Block Party (*Pittsburgh Press* reprint)." Fitzgerald, Francis J., ed. *Greatest Moments in Pittsburgh Steelers History*. Louisville, Ky.: AdCraft Sports Marketing, 1996.

Cope, Myron. "Kiss the Guy or Tackle Him?" (*Saturday Evening Post* reprint, 1963) Roberts, Randy and David Welky, eds. *The Steelers Reader*. Pittsburgh, Pa.: University of Pittsburgh Press, 2001.

Cope, Myron. "The Steelers: Pro Football's Gashouse Gang (*True*, Sept. 1964 reprint)." Fitzgerald, Francis J., ed. *Greatest Moments in Pittsburgh Steelers History*. Louisville, Ky.: AdCraft Sports Marketing, 1996.

Daly, Dan. "Johnny Blood: Before Hall-Raising Came into Vogue, His "Unfettered" Style was NFL Legend." (*Washington Times* reprint) Roberts, Randy and David Welky, eds. *The Steelers Reader*. Pittsburgh, Pa.: University of Pittsburgh Press, 2001.

Danyluk, Tom. "An Interview with Art Rooney, Jr.—Director of Player Personnel/Vice-President Pittsburgh Steelers, Part 1." *The Coffin Corner*, Vol. 28, No. 3, 2006: 3-5, 7-8.

Danyluk, Tom. "An Interview with Art Rooney, Jr.—Director of Player Personnel/Vice-President Pittsburgh Steelers, Part 2." *The Coffin Corner*, Vol. 28, No. 4, 2006: 12.

Didinger, Ray. *Pittsburgh Steelers*. New York: Macmillan Publishing Co., Inc., 1974.

DiMeglio, Steve. "Media day hardly a three-ring circus." *USA Today*. 1 Feb. 2006: 6C.

Dulac, Gerry. "Pittsburgh's Love Affair with the Steelers." Fitzgerald,

Bibliography

Francis J., ed. *Greatest Moments in Pittsburgh Steelers History*. Louisville, Ky.: AdCraft Sports Marketing, 1996.

Dulac, Gerry. "Terry Bradshaw." *Sporting News Selects Pro Football's Greatest Quarterbacks*. Reeves, Barry and Ron Smith, eds. St. Louis, Mo.: *The Sporting News*, 2005: 81.

Duroska, Lud. "Bobby Layne." *Great Pro Quarterbacks*. New York: Grosset & Dunlap, 1972.

Durso, Joseph. "Len Dawson." *Great Pro Quarterbacks*. New York: Grosset & Dunlap, 1972.

Dvorchak, Robert. "Blast from the Past." (*Pittsburgh Post-Gazette*, Dec. 17, 2000, reprint) Roberts, Randy and David Welky, eds. *The Steelers Reader*. Pittsburgh, Pa.: University of Pittsburgh Press, 2001.

Halvonik, Steve. "Art Rooney: A Legend in the NFL and in Life (*Pittsburgh Post-Gazette* reprint)." Fitzgerald, Francis J., ed. *Greatest Moments in Pittsburgh Steelers History*. Louisville, Ky.: AdCraft Sports Marketing, 1996.

Herndon, Booton. *Football's Greatest Quarterbacks*. New York: Bartholomew House, Inc., 1961.

Hogrogian, John. "Byron White's Rookie Season." *The Coffin Corner*, Vol. XVIII, No. 6, 1996: 6, 9, 13, 15.

Horrigan, Joe. "Mike Webster: The Iron Man." *The Coffin Corner*, Vol. XIX, No. 2, 1997: 14-16.

Horrigan, Joe. "Lynn Swann." *The Coffin Corner*, Vol. 23, No. 3, 2001: 15-17.

Horrigan, Joe. "Dan Rooney: Pro Football Hall of Fame Class of 2000." *The Coffin Corner*, Vol. 22, No. 4, 2000: 14-15.

Hubbard, Steve. "Gritty Steelers Bounced by Broncos, 24-23 (*Pittsburgh Press* reprint)." Fitzgerald, Francis J., ed. *Greatest Moments in Pittsburgh Steelers History*. Louisville, Ky.: AdCraft Sports Marketing, 1996.

Hubbard, Steve. "Hoge Has Huge Run of Success (*Pittsburgh Press* reprint)." Fitzgerald, Francis J., ed. *Greatest Moments in Pittsburgh Steelers History*. Louisville, Ky.: AdCraft Sports Marketing, 1996.

Infield, Tom. "When the Steagles Roamed on Gridiron." (*Philadelphia Inquirer* reprint, 1993.) Roberts, Randy and David Welky, eds. *The Steelers Reader*. Pittsburgh, Pa.: University of Pittsburgh Press, 2001.

Johnson. Chuck. "Big Ben takes big stage." *USA TODAY*. 1 Feb. 2006: 1C.

Johnson. Chuck. "Stevens lights fire under Porter: Steelers linebacker takes off gloves in pregame chatter." *USA TODAY*. 2 Feb. 2006: 8C.

King, Peter. "Scoreboard: Monday Morning Quarterback." *Sports Illustrated*, 23 Jan. 2006: 28.

Lambert, Frank. "Reflections on the Pre-Renaissance Steelers." (from *Pittsburgh Stories: Stories from the Steel City*, reprint, 2000.) Roberts, Randy and David Welky, eds. *The Steelers Reader*. Pittsburgh, Pa.: University of Pittsburgh Press, 2001.

Leuthner, Stuart. "Ref, He's Holding!" (from *Iron Men: Bucko, Crazylegs, and the Boys recall the Golden Days of Professional Football*, Doubleday, 1988.) Roberts, Randy and David Welky, eds. *The Steelers Reader*. Pittsburgh, Pa.: University of Pittsburgh Press, 2001.

Livingston, Pat. *The Pittsburgh Steelers: A Pictorial History*. Virginia Beach, Va.: Jordan & Company, Publishers, Inc., 1980.

Livingston, Pat. "Steelers 63, Giants 7: Hard to Believe, Isn't It? (*Pittsburgh Press* reprint)" Fitzgerald, Francis J., ed. *Greatest Moments in Pittsburgh Steelers History*. Louisville, Ky.: AdCraft Sports Marketing, 1996.

Livingston, Pat. "Layne, Orr Team Up to Rip Cardinals, 38-21 (*Pittsburgh Press* reprint)." Fitzgerald, Francis J., ed. *Greatest Moments in Pittsburgh Steelers History*. Louisville, Ky.: AdCraft Sports Marketing, 1996.

Livingston, Pat. "Johnson Runs Wild, Steelers Shock Browns (*Pittsburgh Press* reprint)." Fitzgerald, Francis J., ed. *Greatest Moments in Pittsburgh Steelers History*. Louisville, Ky.: AdCraft Sports Marketing, 1996.

Livingston, Pat. "Definitely the Team of the '70s (*Pittsburgh Press* reprint)." Fitzgerald, Francis J., ed. *Greatest Moments in Pittsburgh Steelers History*. Louisville, Ky.: AdCraft Sports Marketing, 1996.

Livingston, Pat. "Two Keys: Noll, Anderson (*Pittsburgh Press* reprint)." Fitzgerald, Francis J., ed. *Greatest Moments in Pittsburgh Steelers History*. Louisville, Ky.: AdCraft Sports Marketing, 1996.

Matz, Eddie. "Job One." *ESPN The Magazine*. 5 Dec. 2005: 126.

Mendelson. Abby. *The Pittsburgh Steelers: The Official Team History*. Dallas, Texas: Taylor Publishing Company, 1996.

Moyer, Susan M., ed. *Roethlisberger: Pittsburgh's Own Big Ben*. Champaign, Ill.: Sports Publishing LLC, 2004.

Murphy, Austin. "Tough as Nails." *Sports Illustrated: Special NFL Classic Edition*. Volume 83, No. 15, Fall 1995: 22-23, 72.

Musick, Phil. "Steelers on Verge of 1st Title in Club History (*Pittsburgh Press* reprint)." Fitzgerald, Francis J., ed. *Greatest Moments in Pittsburgh Steelers History*. Louisville, Ky.: AdCraft Sports Marketing, 1996.

Musick, Phil. "Steelers Capture First Championship, 24-2 (*Pittsburgh Press* reprint)." Fitzgerald, Francis J., ed. *Greatest Moments in Pittsburgh Steelers History*. Louisville, Ky.: AdCraft Sports Marketing, 1996.

Musick, Phil. "Immaculate Reception Saves the Steelers (*Pittsburgh Press* reprint)." Fitzgerald, Francis J., ed. *Greatest Moments in Pittsburgh Steelers History*. Louisville, Ky.: AdCraft Sports Marketing, 1996.

Musick, Phil. "Bradshaw, Steelers Looking Simply Super (*Pittsburgh Press* reprint)." Fitzgerald, Francis J., ed. *Greatest Moments in Pittsburgh Steelers History*. Louisville, Ky.: AdCraft Sports Marketing, 1996.

Musick, Phil. "Steelers on Cloud IX with Super Win (*Pittsburgh Press* reprint)." Fitzgerald, Francis J., ed. *Greatest Moments in Pittsburgh Steelers History*. Louisville, Ky.: AdCraft Sports Marketing, 1996.

Musick, Phil. "Steelers Dust Off Colts with Defense, 28-10 (*Pittsburgh Press* reprint)." Fitzgerald, Francis J., ed. *Greatest Moments in Pittsburgh Steelers History*. Louisville, Ky.: AdCraft Sports Marketing, 1996.

Musick, Phil. "Steelers 2nd Straight Title Was Just Super (*Pittsburgh Press* reprint)." Fitzgerald, Francis J., ed. *Greatest Moments in Pittsburgh Steelers History*. Louisville, Ky.: AdCraft Sports Marketing, 1996.

Oates, Robert Jr. *Pittsburgh's Steelers: The First Half Century*. Los Angeles: Rosebud Books, 1982.

O'Brien, Jim. "Fans Push Steelers Past Dolphins, 34-14 (*Pittsburgh Press* reprint)." Fitzgerald, Francis J., ed. *Greatest Moments in Pittsburgh Steelers History*. Louisville, Ky.: AdCraft Sports Marketing, 1996.

O'Brien, Jim. *Always a Steeler*. Pittsburgh, Pa.: James P. O'Brien Publishing, 2003.

Olderman, Murray. *The Pro Quarterback*. Englewood Cliffs, N.J.: Prentice-Hall, Inc., 1966.

O'Toole, Andrew. *Smiling Irish Eyes: Art Rooney and the Pittsburgh Steelers*. Haworth, N.J.: St. Johann Press, 2004.

Pedulla, Tom. "Steelers don't cower in doubt." *USA TODAY*. 12 Dec. 2005: 1C.

Pedulla, Tom. "'Big Snack' satisfying: Steelers love anchor Hampton." *USA TODAY*. 1 Feb. 2006: 4C.

Pedulla, Tom. "MVP Ward produces crucial yards at opportune times." *USA TODAY*. 6 Feb. 2006: 1C.

Povich. Shirley. "Senior Citizen of the Pittsburgh Steelers." (*Washington Post* reprint) Roberts, Randy and David Welky, eds. *The Steelers Reader*. Pittsburgh, Pa.: University of Pittsburgh Press, 2001.

Richman, Michael. "Bill Dudley." *The Coffin Corner*, Vol. 25, No. 4, 2003: 21-22.

Rodenbush, Jim. "Troy Polamalu." *Tough As Steel: Pittsburgh Steelers 2006 Super Bowl Champions*. Champaign, Ill.: Sports Publishing L.L.C./Pittsburgh, Pa.: Tribune-Review Publishing Company, 2006.

Ross, Alan. "The Punters of the Fabulous Fifties." *NFL Insider*, Vol. XXIX No. 4: 8C.

Ross, Alan. "Class Reunion: Another Steeler from Draft Class of '74." *Lindy's 2002 Pro Football*: 115.

Ross, Alan. "No Brain, No Gain: Mental Toughness is the ultimate key to success." *Sporting News Special Collectors' Edition: Pro Football's Tough Guys*. 2003: 71-72.

Ross, Alan. "Mean Joe Greene: 'It's more mental' than physical." *Sporting News Special Collectors' Edition: Pro Football's Tough Guys*. 2003: 30.

Ross, Alan. "The Silver and Black." *Sporting News Special Collectors' Edition: Pro Football's Tough Guys*. 2003: 84.

Ross, Alan. "The Steel Curtain." *Sporting News Special Collectors' Edition: Pro Football's Tough Guys*. 2003: 87.

Bibliography

Sahadi, Lou. *Steelers: Team of the Decade*. New York: Times Books, 1979.

Saraceno, Jon. "Keeping Score: Pick: Steelers by a whisker." *USA TODAY*. 1 Feb. 2006: 4C.

Sargent, Jim. "Frank Varrichione: All-American and Pro Bowl Tackle." *The Coffin Corner*, Vol. XXI, No. 5, 1999: 4, 6.

Sargent, Jim. "The Steelers' Pro Bowl Guard of the Early 1950s." *The Coffin Corner*, Vol. XX, No. 6, 1998: 13-15.

Sheeley, Glenn. "High Flying Steelers Crash Colts, 40-14 (*Pittsburgh Press* reprint)." Fitzgerald, Francis J., ed. *Greatest Moments in Pittsburgh Steelers History*. Louisville, Ky.: AdCraft Sports Marketing, 1996.

Smith, Robert. *Pro Football: The History of the Game and the Great Players*. Garden City, N.Y.: Doubleday & Company, Inc., 1963.

Smizik, Bob. "Let's Not Forget the Great Times at Three Rivers." (*Pittsburgh Post-Gazette*, June 20, 1999, reprint) Roberts, Randy and David Welky, eds. *The Steelers Reader*. Pittsburgh, Pa.: University of Pittsburgh Press, 2001.

Sparrow, Mike. "All-Time Non Pro Bowl Team." *The Coffin Corner*, Vol. XX, No. 1, 1998: 4.

Troup, T.J. "Bullet Bill Dudley and the Steelers of 1942 and 1946." *The Coffin Corner*, Vol.22, No. 6, 2000: 9.

Tucker, Joe. *Steelers' Victory After Forty*. New York: Exposition Press, Inc., 1973.

Vargo. Norm. Stadium Stories: *Pittsburgh Steelers, Colorful Tales of the Black and Gold*. Guilford, Conn.: The Globe Pequot Press, 2005.

Weisman, Larry. "Steelers record Motown hit: Strong 2nd half gives Pittsburgh one for thumb." *USA TODAY*. 6 Feb. 2006: 2C.

Wexell, Jim. *Tales from Behind the Steel Curtain*. Champaign, Ill.: Sports Publishing, L.L.C., 2004.

Zimmerman, Paul. "They Were Just Too Much." (*Sports Illustrated*, Jan. 28, 1980, reprint) Roberts, Randy and David Welky, eds. *The Steelers Reader*. Pittsburgh, Pa.: University of Pittsburgh Press, 2001.

WEB SITES

Associated Press. "Bettis headed home for first Super Bowl." http://sports.espn.go.com/nfl/playoffs05/news/story?id=2302302, Jan. 22, 2006.

Associated Press. "Steelers stalwart, longtime Cowboys coordinator dies." http://sports.espn.go.com/nfl/news/story?id=2332769, Feb. 16, 2006.

Associated Press. "Big Ben apologizes, pledges he'll ride wearing helmet." http://sports.espn.go.com/nfl/news/story?id=2484472, June 15, 2006.

Associated Press. "Big Ben to be cited for riding without helmet, permit." http://sports.espn.go.com/nfl/news/story?id=2490987, June 19, 2006.

Bell, Jarrett and Nate Davis, et al. "Detroit is cut in Steelers' cloth." USA

Today.com. http://www.usatoday.com/sports/football/super/2006-02-05-notes_x.htm, Feb. 6, 2006.

Bouchette, Ed. "Steelers/NFL: Steelers, Bengals rivalry heats up." Post-Gazette.com Sports. http://post-gazette.com/pg/06088/677630-66.stm, Mar. 29, 2006.

Davis, Nate. "Porter's final shot at Stevens has a true ring." USA Today .com. http://www.usatoday.com/sports/football/super/2006-02-05-porter _x.htm, Feb. 6, 2006.

Emert, Rich. "Where are they now?: Jon Kolb." Tri-State Sports & News Service. Post-Gazette.com. http://www.post-gazette.com/steelers/ 20010913where0914p5.asp, Sept. 13, 2001.

Famous Quotes. www.steelersfever.com. http://www.steelersfever.com/ quotes.html.

Football Quotes. www.ffbookmarks.com. http://www.ffbookmarks.com/ football_quotes.htm.

Football Steelers Community. footballhuddles.com. http://footballhuddles .com/vbulletin/showthread.php?s=ae3e77de021592cd424e58b812f60471 &threadid=23734.

Garber, Greg. "Winning for Bettis motivates Steelers." ESPN.com. http://sports.espn.go.com/nfl/playoffs05/news/story?id=2310874, Jan. 29, 2006.

Garber, Greg. "Bettis drives off in style." ESPN.com. http://sports. espn.go.com/nfl/playoffs05/news/story?id=2320642, Feb. 6, 2006.

Google Groups. "Craig Heyward rambles no more." http://groups. google.co.uk/group/rsfcmoderated/browse_thread/thread/a260bdefc8f7 f7b8/87b0071be23fe9e0, June 5, 2006.

Hines Ward quotes. thinkexist.com. http://en.thinkexist.com/quotes/ hines_ward/.

Hooper, Ernest. "Baltimore's Rod Woodson: The safety is on." *St. Petersburg Times*. http://www.sptimes.com/News/012001/SuperBowl2001/ Baltimore_s_Rod_Woods.shtml, Jan. 20, 2001.

Johnson, Chuck. "Parker sprint sets Steelers on right track." USA Today.com. http://www.usatoday.com/sports/football/nfl/steelers/2006-02-06-parker_x.htm, Feb. 6, 2006.

Sean Keeler. "Rivalry steep in tradition." cincypost.com. http://www.cincypost.com/bengals/2001/beng100601.html, Oct. 6, 2001.

NFL.com. "NFL News: Rivalry Week Is Here." http://www.nfl.com/ news/story/5701596, Sept. 10, 2002.

NFL.com wire reports. "Steelers survive strange Colts rally, 21-18." http://www.nfl.com/gamecenter/recap/NFL_20060115_PIT@IND, Jan. 15, 2006.

Official web site of Ernie Stautner. http://www.cmgworldwide. com/football/stautner/index.html.

Pasquarelli, Len. "Second-year QB flawless for Detroit-bound Steelers."

Bibliography

ESPN.com. http://sports.espn.go.com/nfl/playoffs05/columns/story? columnist=pasquarelli_len&id=2302464, Jan. 22, 2006.

Pittsburgh Post Gazette, "Arthur J. Rooney, 1901-88," reprinted on http://www.pittsburghsteelers.co.uk/steelers/rooneys/page1.htm, Aug. 30, 1998.

Saraceno, Jon. "Cowher can rest easy with title finally in hand." USA Today.com. http://www.usatoday.com/sports/columnist/saraceno/2006-02-06-cowher_x.htm, Feb. 6, 2006.

Sargent, Jim. "Lynn Chandnois: The Steeler 'Money' Back of the 1950s." http://www.footballresearch.com/articles/frpage.cfm?topic=chandnois.

Smith, Michael. "Road-tested Steelers cruise into Motown." ESPN.com. http://sports.espn.go.com/nfl/playoffs05/columns/story?columnist =smith_michael&id=2302485, Jan. 22, 2006.

Tanier, Mike. "Too Deep Zone: Hines 57." www.footballoutsiders.com. http://www.footballoutsiders.com/2006/01/27/ramblings/too-deep-zone/3586/, Jan. 27, 2006.

Wojciechowski, Gene. "Super moments make Super Bowl XL memorable." ESPN.com. http://sports.espn.go.com/espn/columns/story?columnist=wojciechowski_gene&id=2320685, Feb. 5, 2006.

Wojciechowski, Gene. "Roethlisberger's next ad? Wear a helmet." ESPN.com.http://sports.espn.go.com/espn/columns/story?columnist=wojciechowski_gene&id=2482497&lpos=spotlight&lid=tab5pos1, June 13, 2006.

Wickersham, Seth. "Former QB hits Ward for game-clinching TD." ESPN.com. http://sports.espn.go.com/nfl/playoffs05/news/story?id=2320690, Feb. 5, 2006.

PERSONAL INTERVIEWS:

Creekmur, Lou. May 28, 2002
Greene, Joe. May 4, 2003.
Ham, Jack. May 14, 2003
Hannah, John. March 14, 2003.
Hendricks, Ted. May 13, 2003
Stallworth, John. March 5, 2002
Upshaw, Gene. May 13, 2003

INDEX

Index

Index

Index